Graveyard London

First published 2008
by Historical Publications Ltd
32 Ellington Street, London N7 8PL
(Tel: 020 7607 1628)

ISBN 978-1-905286-25-6
British Library Cataloguing-in-Publication Data
A catalogue record for this book is available from the British Library

Typeset in Book Antiqua by Historical Publications Ltd
Reproduction by Tintern Graphics
Printed by Edelvives, Zaragoza, Spain

The Illustrations

All the illustrations were supplied by the author, with the exception of the following:

Leslie Abrahams: *22, 76, 77, 97, 104, 128, 130*
Guildhall Library, Corporation of London: *100*
Historical Publications Ltd: *16, 20, 23, 30, 31, 36, 42, 54, 56, 66, 71, 74, 78, 80, 83, 94, 99, 101*
London Metropolitan Archives: *159*
Museum of London Archaeological Service: *6, 7, 10, 13, 14, 114, 153*
David Orme: *112*
Ruth Richardson: *2*
The Wellcome Trust: *4*

The front jacket illustration is *A Grave Idea* by T. Jones, 1828, reproduced by kind permission of V & A Images, Victoria & Albert Museum, London.
The back jacket illustration (and title page decoration) is an invitation to a funeral, designed by William Hogarth (1697-1764) for the undertaker Humphrey Drew of King Street, Westminster.

Graveyard London

Lost and forgotten burial grounds

Robert Bard

HISTORICAL PUBLICATIONS

CONTENTS

ACKNOWLEDGEMENTS

There are a number of people without whom this book would not have been possible. Leslie Abrahams not only acted as a researcher, but as well by his determination never to give up when lost burial grounds did seem truly lost, he has added much by way of information and photography to this book. I could not have written *Graveyard London* without his assistance.

Children's author and fellow enthusiast, David Orme, allowed me access and use of his website http:www.doubleo.fsnet.co.uk, which contains a comprehensive record of London's burial grounds. David offered information and humour when being telephoned on a number of occasions from central London with a plea to use Google Earth to locate a couple of the more obscure burial grounds, which should have been where I was, but were not. He assisted greatly by answering my many burial ground enquiries.

I would also like to thank Vanessa Harding for allowing me to quote some pertinent paragraphs from her publications on plague burials.

John Richardson made valuable additions to the manuscript, and as well removed some burial grounds that were 'neither lost nor hidden!'

INTRODUCTION

It is a fascinating thought that many hundreds of generations of Londoners lie beneath the city without us knowing. Through centuries burial grounds have been developed, built over, and then forgotten. Occasionally when modern development takes place, remains are disturbed and we are reminded of a London that has long since disappeared. This re-emergence of burial grounds is not a new phenomenon – the London historian, John Stow (*c.* 1525-1605), in his *Survey of London* (1598), remarked upon bones that were unearthed in 1576 at Spitalfields. The purpose of this book, with the aid of four walks, is to identify some of those lost or forgotten burial grounds of central London.

A history of some aspects of London published in 1862 observed that:

> ... an interesting chapter might be written on the London Churchyards and Burial-places now closed under the provisions of the salutary enactment for extramural interment of the dead. Not strangers only, but residents in the metropolis have little idea of the prodigious mass of human remains accumulated in neighbourhoods now densely populated, and in close contiguity to the great thoroughfares and resorts of business and amusement. Some startling facts on this subject, as regards the City churchyards, and shewing that the centre of London life may be considered one vast necropolis, are revealed in a Report recently made by Dr.Letherby, the officer of health. Besides the existing churchyards, numerous others are built over, or levelled and thrown into streets and public places.[1]

The digging of railway lines and tube tunnels, from Victorian times to the present, led to the discovery of forgotten burial grounds. Plague pits from the hurried mass burials of the 14th to 17th centuries occasionally come to light. This has interested generations of London historians. Indeed, in the 1880s a Mrs Basil Holmes observed 'In looking one day at Rocque's plan of London [*c.* 1746] I noticed how many burial-grounds and churchyards were marked upon it which no longer existed ... I commenced to draw up a list of all the burying-places, of which I could find any record, still existing, or that had ever existed in London. It was no easy task.'[2]

By the use of 'ancient and modern maps' and visiting the sites she identified many such as 'the German ground in the Savoy, the additional ground to St Martin-in-the-Fields, and Thomas' ground in Golden Lane ...' all of which had disappeared. As a middle-class Victorian woman she tells us that she had some fascinating experiences whilst out 'graveyards-hunting.' Twice she had mud thrown at her 'once by a woman in Cable Street ... and once by a man in Silchester Road.' At the time, with research at the British Museum and the use of 60 Ordnance Survey maps, Holmes identified within the 'County and City of London' 362 burial grounds of which 41 were still in use. A further 90 had become public gardens and playgrounds. This number excluded churches and chapels with vaults under them. Thus began an extensive work which looked at all categories of burial grounds ranging from Roman interments, to 'Pest-Fields and Plague Pits' and many more. The result of this extensive survey was a 'List of Burial-Grounds in Existence' and 'Burial-Grounds which have disappeared'.

Her findings were encapsulated in a book entitled *The London Burial Grounds*, published in 1896. It was no accident that Mrs Holmes should be the author of this unique work. She had been the first secretary of the Metropolitan Public Gardens Association (MPGA) when it was formed in 1882 under the chairmanship of Earl Meath (Reginald Brabazon), and her husband, Basil, was her successor as secretary from 1887 to 1937. The Association was one of the most successful lobbying organisations in London during that period and involved itself in at least 1000 schemes for public spaces which included the saving of old burial grounds, especially those attached to central London churches.

Isabella Holmes was no 'spare woman'. She was a daughter of Dr J H Gladstone, a notable Sandemanian minister (a Christian sect originating in Scotland), and a sister of Florence Gladstone, historian of Kensington and Notting Hill. She worked energetically for the MPGA for at least fifty years, during which time the Association could claim to be very influential indeed in the saving of Kenwood, the Geffrye Museum in Shoreditch and numerous public squares, commons and open spaces at a time when development loomed. The Association not only obtained the passing of the Disused Burial Grounds Act of 1884, which put all burial grounds 'outside the class of eligible building sites', but also helped to promote another organisation that fought the building over of London squares. Their most notable loss was that of the gardens of Mornington Crescent in Camden Town, but otherwise Londoners owe this energetic and dedicated couple, whose names are hardly known today, an enormous debt. Basil Holmes also found time to be an outspoken proponent of daylight saving.

Mrs Holmes died in Hastings on 6 June 1949, aged 87. Her husband died on 28 January 1940, aged 83.

Mrs Holmes identifies a cycle of use relating to burial grounds which still holds true when she says that 'it is interesting to trace on maps of different dates the rise and fall of a graveyard. First there is the actual field, which on some particular day was acquired for the purpose. Then there is the burial-ground formed and in use. Then the plot appears to be vacant – put to no purpose, or used as a yard. Lastly buildings are on it, and the graveyard has quite disappeared.'[3]

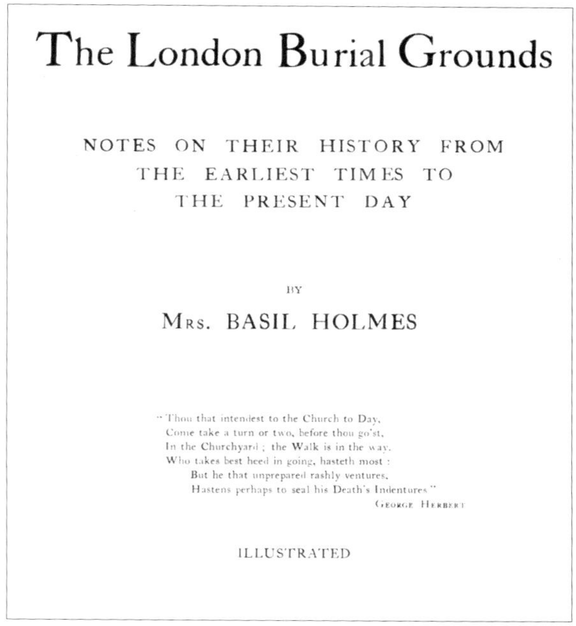
The London Burial Grounds

NOTES ON THEIR HISTORY FROM THE EARLIEST TIMES TO THE PRESENT DAY

BY

MRS. BASIL HOLMES

"Thou that intendest to the Church to Day,
Come take a turn or two, before thou go'st,
In the Churchyard ; the Walk is in the way.
Who takes best heed in going, hasteth most :
But he that unprepared rashly ventures,
Hastens perhaps to seal his Death's Indentures"
GEORGE HERBERT

ILLUSTRATED

1. The frontispiece to Mrs Basil Holmes' London Burial Grounds, published in 1896.

Holmes based some of her work on publications by a doctor, George Alfred Walker (1808-84), who exposed in a succession of reports the unhygienic and overcrowded state of many of London's churchyards and burial-grounds. Not only does he describe their condition but he revealed the practices often carried out by owners of many private chapels and grounds, which involved the destruction of newly buried coffins and remains in order to cram more into the same piece of ground.

Walker was to become a prominent campaigner against burials within areas of dense human habitation. His own surgery was located at 101 Drury Lane, close to the St Martin's Drury Lane burial ground, a ground so overflowing with bodies that the graveyard became 'level with the first floor windows surrounding the place.'[4] Against much vested opposition, Walker believed that the emanations from London's overcrowded burial grounds were dangerous to

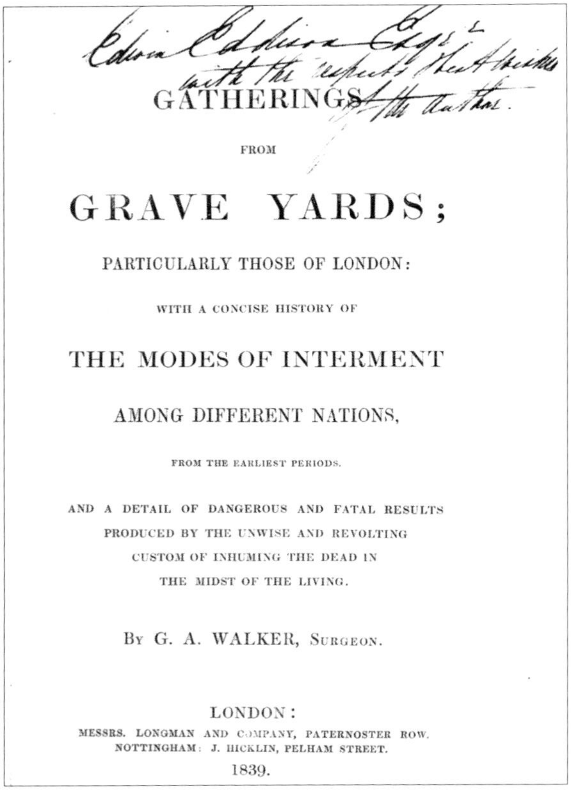
GATHERINGS

FROM

GRAVE YARDS;

PARTICULARLY THOSE OF LONDON:

WITH A CONCISE HISTORY OF

THE MODES OF INTERMENT

AMONG DIFFERENT NATIONS,

FROM THE EARLIEST PERIODS.

AND A DETAIL OF DANGEROUS AND FATAL RESULTS
PRODUCED BY THE UNWISE AND REVOLTING
CUSTOM OF INHUMING THE DEAD IN
THE MIDST OF THE LIVING.

BY G. A. WALKER, SURGEON.

LONDON:
MESSRS. LONGMAN AND COMPANY, PATERNOSTER ROW.
NOTTINGHAM: J. HICKLIN, PELHAM STREET.
1839.

2. *The frontispiece of George Walker's* Gatherings from Grave Yards, *published in 1839. It is dedicated by the author. (Courtesy Ruth Richardson)*

the health of those who lived in the vicinity. There was published in rapid succession a spate of Walker publications, all dedicated to the ending of metropolitan intra and extra mural interments. These were, *Gatherings from Grave Yards* in 1839, *The Grave Yards of London* in 1841, *Interment and Disinterment*, 1843, *Burial Ground Incendiarism* in 1846 and in 1847 a series of lectures on the actual conditions of the Metropolitan Graveyards. The flavour of Walker's style can be gained from the introduction to his magnificently titled 1846 document '*Spa-Fields Golgotha, Last Fire at the Bone-House in the Spa-Fields Golgotha, or, The Minute Anatomy of Grave-Digging.*

Walker quotes another doctor and begins:

No burying-places should be tolerated within cities or towns, much less in or about CHURCHES and CHAPELS. This custom is excessively injurious to the inhabitants, and especially to those who frequent public worship in such CHAPELS and CHURCHES. God, decency and health forbid this shocking abomination *** From long observation I can attest that CHURCHES and CHAPELS situated in grave-yards, and those especially within whose walls the dead are interred, are perfectly unwholesome; and many, by attending such places, are shortening their passage to the house appointed for the living. What increases the iniquity of this abominable and deadly work is, that the burying-grounds attached to many CHURCHES and CHAPELS are made a source of PRIVATE GAIN. The whole of this preposterous conduct is as indecorous and unhealthy as it is profane...[5]

Spa Fields, located in Clerkenwell, was one of London's most overcrowded private burial grounds, and will be looked at in chapter three. Two more, also dealt with later, were a burial ground and chapel in Globe Fields, Whitechapel (the ground partly survives), and the Enon Chapel in Aldwych, which now lies beneath part of the London School of Economics.

Evidence of other grounds described by both Walker and Holmes is still clear in the playgrounds of schools, many of which were built over or beside them, and in central London a surprisingly large number of people live in proximity to them without realising the significance of the hillocks and bumps in the ground. The majority of those interred up until modern times had no coffin, gravestone or marker. In researching this book I found burial grounds still not built on, but preserved as courtyards to council flats, or acting as gardens to rows of houses. Some of them are apparent if you are looking for them, but the majority need a sharp eye and a copy of an 18th- or 19th-century map.

Holmes reminds us that history lies buried in some of London's most famous landmarks. After the Great Fire of 1666, when Wren undertook the rebuilding of many of London's churches, he came upon the layered remains of Londoners reaching back in some cases to Roman times. Holmes reproduces a contemporary report (Wren's 'Parentalia') of such finds when he rebuilt St Paul's Cathedral:

> Upon digging the foundation of the present fabric of St Paul's, he found under the graves of the latter ages, in a row below them, the Burial-places of the Saxon times – the Saxons, as it appeared, were accustomed to line their graves with chalk-stones, though some more eminent were entombed in coffins of whole stones. Below these were British graves, where they found ivory and wooden pins, of a hard wood, seemingly box, in abundance, of about six inches long; it seems the bodies were only wrapped up, and pinned in woollen shrouds, which being consumed, the pins remained entire. In the same ground, and deeper, were Roman urns intermixed. This was eighteen feet deep or more, and belonged to the colony when Romans and Britons lived and died together.

The Black Death of 1349 required the allocation of large areas of land for burials. A number of these plague sites will be looked at. The Great Plague of 1665, with deaths sometimes at a level of 4000 per week, put extraordinary pressure on churchyards, leading to overflowing and highly unsanitary conditions. This resulted then in the creation of new burial grounds, one of which was the Dissenters' ground, Bunhill Fields in Finsbury, which was not completed until 1666. There is some uncertainty as to whether this burial ground was actually used for plague victims. In the 19th century, development in the area of Marble Arch, particularly Connaught Place and Bryanston Street, led to the unearthing of human remains – the workmen had recovered some of the many thousands of victims of the Tyburn gallows, buried in pits near their place of execution. Somewhere near the corner of Oxford Street and the Edgware Road possibly lie the remains of three of the regicides responsible for the execution of Charles I, including Oliver Cromwell, which, at the Restoration, were dug up from their original burial places and hanged at Tyburn.

Many of London's burial grounds now survive as City of London gardens. Holmes tells us for example that the burial ground of 'the priory of St Augustine Papey survives in the little churchyard of the former St Martin Outwich in Camomile Street, on the corner of Threadneedle Street and Bishopsgate, which was presented to the parish by Robert Hyde in 1538 ...' When the vaults of this church were cleared the remains included those of a Mrs Abigail Vaughan, who left 4s a year to buy faggots to burn heretics.

The gardens of the City churches, often the former burial grounds, have been the subject of a number of excellent books. This present work therefore will look primarily at some of those burial grounds, mainly north of the Thames, that have disappeared beneath modern developments, or remain but are difficult to identify without the aid of an appropriate map and an inquisitive nature. Some remain unmarked as courtyards, or ominously humped play areas for children. I have included church burial grounds and crypts where Holmes has mentioned them, or where they are interesting within the general theme of this book. The many remaining lost and hidden burial grounds north of the Thames, and those to the south, of which there are many, will have to await a further volume.

An unhealthy stench

The consequence of the shortage of burial space and the overflowing churchyards was that burials were shallow and often haphazard. Descriptions abound of the stench emanating from beneath the floors of churches, around the churchyards, and in some cases schools that had vaults crammed with remains directly beneath. The hazard to health was such that Parliament stepped in with statutes relating to burials. It was during the period of the 1840s-1870s that increasing use was made of dedicated cemeteries on the periphery of London which were either privately owned or else related to specific parishes. Some of these were designed as gardens and many are now tourist attractions. Kensal Green Cemetery opened in January of

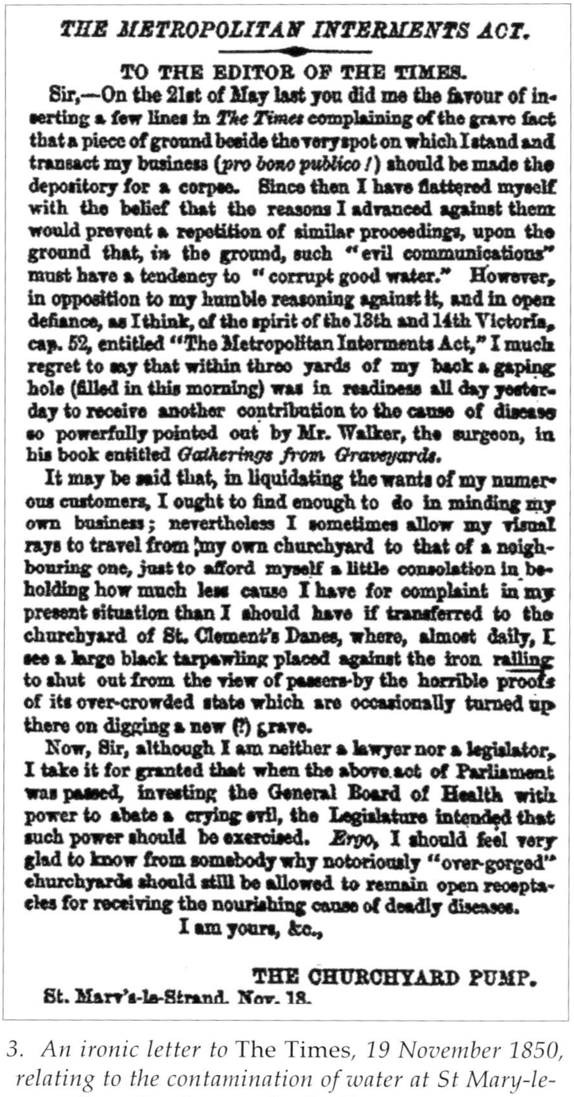

THE METROPOLITAN INTERMENTS ACT.

TO THE EDITOR OF THE TIMES.

Sir,—On the 21st of May last you did me the favour of inserting a few lines in *The Times* complaining of the grave fact that a piece of ground beside the very spot on which I stand and transact my business (*pro bono publico!*) should be made the depository for a corpse. Since then I have flattered myself with the belief that the reasons I advanced against them would prevent a repetition of similar proceedings, upon the ground that, *in* the ground, such "evil communications" must have a tendency to "corrupt good water." However, in opposition to my humble reasoning against it, and in open defiance, as I think, of the spirit of the 13th and 14th Victoria, cap. 52, entitled "The Metropolitan Interments Act," I much regret to say that within three yards of my back a gaping hole (filled in this morning) was in readiness all day yesterday to receive another contribution to the cause of disease so powerfully pointed out by Mr. Walker, the surgeon, in his book entitled *Gatherings from Graveyards.*

It may be said that, in liquidating the wants of my numerous customers, I ought to find enough to do in minding my own business; nevertheless I sometimes allow my visual rays to travel from my own churchyard to that of a neighbouring one, just to afford myself a little consolation in beholding how much less cause I have for complaint in my present situation than I should have if transferred to the churchyard of St. Clement's Danes, where, almost daily, I see a large black tarpawling placed against the iron railing to shut out from the view of passers-by the horrible proofs of its over-crowded state which are occasionally turned up there on digging a new (?) grave.

Now, Sir, although I am neither a lawyer nor a legislator, I take it for granted that when the above act of Parliament was passed, investing the General Board of Health with power to abate a crying evil, the Legislature intended that such power should be exercised. *Ergo*, I should feel very glad to know from somebody why notoriously "over-gorged" churchyards should still be allowed to remain open receptacles for receiving the nourishing cause of deadly diseases.

I am yours, &c.,

THE CHURCHYARD PUMP.

St. Mary's-le-Strand. Nov. 18.

3. *An ironic letter to* The Times, *19 November 1850, relating to the contamination of water at St Mary-le-Strand and at nearby St Clement Danes.*

1833, Norwood in 1837, Highgate in 1839, Brompton in 1840. Campaigns against the state of London's burial grounds, made urgent by serious cholera outbreaks, resulted in a series of Acts which began with the 1852 Metropolitan Burial Act which prohibited burials in central London. Bunhill Fields, which contained the graves of approximately 120,000 Londoners, including William Blake, John Bunyan and Daniel Defoe, became a public open space in 1867.

Walker and Holmes make apparent how haphazard and indifferent many interments were. Burial today is efficiently, hygienically and respectfully organised but in the 19th century passers-by of some of London's better known churches might witness churchyards littered with scraps of coffins and decaying human remains. St Mary's church on the Whitechapel Road, which now survives only as a white marked outline in the grass, surrounded by a scattering of tombstones, was described in 1839 by Walker as abutting 'upon one of the greatest thoroughfares in London ... its appearance altogether is extremely disgusting, and I have no doubt that the putrefactive process which is here very rapidly going on, must, in a great measure, be the cause of producing, certainly of increasing, the numerous diseases by which the lower order of the inhabitants of this parish have so frequently been visited.' He continues:

> The ground is so densely crowded as to present one entire mass of human bones and putrefaction which are in the course of further interments exhumed by the shovelfuls, and disgustingly exposed to the pensive observations of the passer-by ... to the jeers or contempt of the profane or brutal ... most of the graves are very shallow, some entire coffins, indeed, are to be found within a foot and a half of the surface.[6]

The East End of London was by no means unusual. St Anne's Soho boasted a churchyard where graves were kept open in 'expectancy' and Walker reports that 'rotten coffin wood and fragments are scattered about.'[7] Even churchyards such as that of St Margaret's Westminster, under the nose of Parliament and adjacent to Westminster Abbey, which today presents a picture of cultivated greenery and propriety, caused disquiet and was full to saturation point. Sir Edwin Chadwick, Public Health Commissioner 1848-1854, carried out a burial ground survey there in 1841:

> Again, where the drainage of the district in which the church may be placed is of an inferior description, and liable to be impeded periodically by the state of the

tide, as in the vicinity of the Houses of Parliament, where all the drains are closed at high water, the atmosphere is frequently of the most inferior quality. I am fully satisfied, for instance, not only from my own observation, but from different statements that have reached me, and also from the observations of parties who have repeatedly examined the subject at my request, that the state of the burying-ground around St Margaret's church is prejudicial to the air supplied at the Houses of Parliament, and also to the whole neighbourhood. One of them, indeed, stated to me lately that he had avoided the churchyard for the last six months, in consequence of the effects he experienced the last time he visited it. These offensive emanations have been noticed at all hours of the night and morning; and even during the day the smell of the churchyard has been considered to have reached the vaults in the House of Commons, and traced to sewers in its immediate vicinity.[8]

The constant burial upon burial in many cases substantially raised the level of the churchyards. The results can be seen today. St Bartholomew the Great in Smithfield has a ground raised several feet above the entrance to the church, as does St Bride's in Fleet Street. A consequence of this overcrowding was sometimes contamination of drinking water because many churchyards contained the local water pump.

Some burial grounds have disappeared beneath railway extensions and office blocks. Some partly remain as recreation grounds, with surviving sections beneath schools or car parks. In researching this volume, it became clear that Holmes' 1896 observation that many burial grounds now lay under schools and playgrounds, is still the case. It is likely that rather than face the problem of mass exhumations associated with redevelopment, the simple alternative after the closure of the metropolitan burial grounds in the 1850s, was to bury them beneath recreation or playgrounds.

Every foray into the centre and suburbs of London armed with Mrs Holmes' book and printed out sections of maps from earlier centuries, provided surprises. Aldgate churchyard, the site of one of London's largest plague pits, and where two gravediggers died in 1838 from inhaling the noxious fumes of putrefaction whilst digging a burial pit, can still be imagined despite the now truncated nature of the Aldgate church burial area.

Much of the enjoyment of the research was in locating small areas of history intact amongst the devastation created by World War II and the advance of office blocks. Many of the lost burial grounds retain an atmosphere of their pasts. Even Whitechapel, severely damaged during the war, yielded grounds in areas where time and war had barely caused harm. My search, aided by two other enthusiasts,[9] was rewarded by a sense of accomplishment and discovery, but also sadness that so many of our forbears lie in unmarked graves, in unmarked grounds, and now totally forgotten. Some lie in the unlikeliest of places. The Aske's Hospital burial ground in Chart Street, Hoxton is situated in the courtyard of a block of council flats. The overflow ground for St Mary's church in Whitechapel lies just behind Whitechapel Road on a housing estate. The only reminder of its past is the height of the ground (see ill. 59) and the tell-tale dips and humps.

1 E Meteyard *The Hallowed Spots of Ancient London* (1862), pp.167-168.
2 Isabella (Mrs Basil) Holmes, *The London Burial Grounds* (1896), p.13.
3 Holmes p.20.
4 George A Walker *Gatherings from Grave Yards* (1839), p.162.
5 George A. Walker, *Burial-ground Incendiarism. The last fire at the Bone-House in the Spa-Fields Golgotha, or the minute anatomy of Grave-digging in London* (1846), Intro p.1.
6 Walker, *Gatherings*, p.168.
7 Walker, *Gatherings*, p.177.
8 Edwin Chadwick, *A report on the results of a special inquiry into the practice of interment in towns, etc,* (1845) ed. by C Sherman, p.41.
9 David Orme and Les Abrahams.

CHAPTER ONE

LONDON BURIALS

Sickening and Horrible

Charles Knight (1791-1873), in his history of London,[1] devotes a chapter to what was then the highly topical subject of burials in London, and the overcrowding of the burial grounds that had degenerated to a stage where health was endangered. He introduces his subject: 'It was on the 8th of March, 1842, that the Committee of the House of Commons was appointed, to which we are indebted for the discovery of a state of things in London which is truly described by one witness as "sickening" and "horrible," and which exhibits England, through its capital (in the words of the Committee's Report), as an "instance of the most wealthy, moral, and civilised community in the world, tolerating a practice and an abuse which has been corrected for years by nearly all other civilised nations in every part of the globe."'[2]

Public Health Commissioner, Sir Edwin Chadwick (1800-90) presented a picture that, although bad, was made worse by the increasing number of private owners who for profit, set up burial grounds for the poor. In his report to the House of Commons in 1845 he wrote:

The most crowded burial grounds, on the average, are, it appears, the grounds which belong to private individuals, usually undertakers. In these places an uneducated man generally acts as minister, puts on a surplice, and reads the church service, or any other service that may be called for. These grounds are morally offensive, and appear to be physically dangerous in proportion to the numbers interred in them. In one of them the numbers interred appears to be at the rate of more than 2,300 per acre per annum. Names are given to these places by the owners, importing connexion with congregations, but without any apparent authority for doing so....'[3]

4. Edwin Chadwick.

The effect of these private burial yards was, as Chadwick reported, that 'in the common grave-yards in the metropolis, the bones are scattered about or wheeled away to a bone-house, where they are thrown in a heap.'[4] Witnesses were called and the report contained some of their evidence. The testimony of Dr Lyon Playfair makes grim reading:

'I know several church-yards from which most foetid smells are evolved, and gases with similar odour are emitted ... The worst burying grounds which have come under my notice are those belonging to private persons, generally undertakers, who make their livelihood by interring at a cheap rate. I visited one of these only a few days since. It was about 150 feet

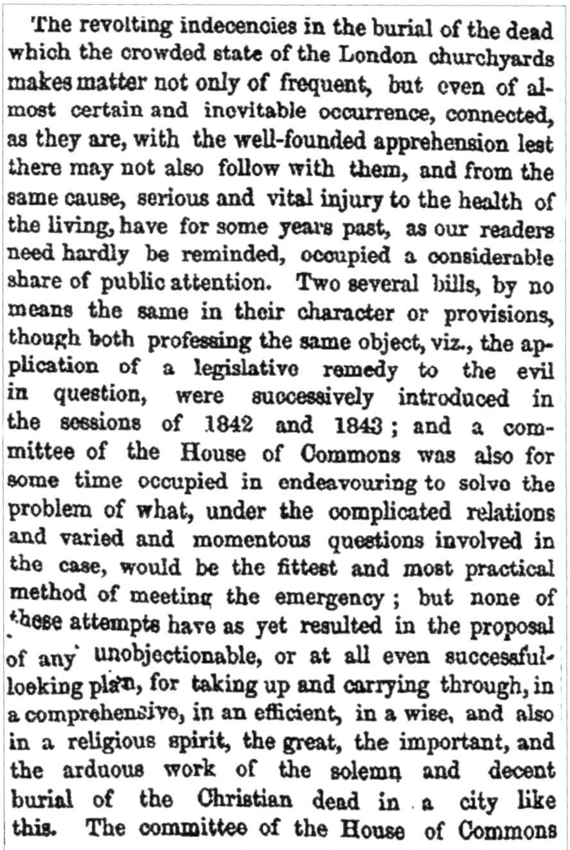

The revolting indecencies in the burial of the dead which the crowded state of the London churchyards makes matter not only of frequent, but even of almost certain and inevitable occurrence, connected, as they are, with the well-founded apprehension lest there may not also follow with them, and from the same cause, serious and vital injury to the health of the living, have for some years past, as our readers need hardly be reminded, occupied a considerable share of public attention. Two several bills, by no means the same in their character or provisions, though both professing the same object, viz., the application of a legislative remedy to the evil in question, were successively introduced in the sessions of 1842 and 1843; and a committee of the House of Commons was also for some time occupied in endeavouring to solve the problem of what, under the complicated relations and varied and momentous questions involved in the case, would be the fittest and most practical method of meeting the emergency; but none of these attempts have as yet resulted in the proposal of any unobjectionable, or at all even successful-looking plan, for taking up and carrying through, in a comprehensive, in an efficient, in a wise, and also in a religious spirit, the great, the important, and the arduous work of the solemn and decent burial of the Christian dead in a city like this. The committee of the House of Commons

5. Editorial in The Times, 22 December 1843, on 'revolting indecencies in the burial of the dead'.

long and about 30 broad, and had been used for 80 years as a burying ground, and was still a favourite place of interment among the poor. Of course many bodies are placed in one grave, and when the ground becomes too much raised by bodies, it is levelled, and the boxes, &c., exhumed during the levelling, are thrown into a large cellar fitted to receive them. This whole ground was a mass of corruption, as well may be supposed, and it is situated in a densely populated neighbourhood. I mention this case as one among many other similar cases of private burying grounds, in order to suggest that attention should be paid in any alteration respecting the laws regulating interments, to prevent burying-grounds being kept as objects of pecuniary speculation, at least within towns; for this practice gives much inducement to violate every feeling of decency and regard for public health in the desire for gain.'[5]

Profits from Death

In the cause of private gain, little was sacrosanct – respect for the dead came a distant second to the financial rewards of burying them. The Anglican and non-conformist churches relied on burial fees to maintain the clergy and they, together with the private burial ground proprietors, saw George Walker as a threat to their livelihoods. He concentrated on bringing a small number of particularly noxious burial grounds to the fore to promote his case. These grounds, which will be looked at in some detail, were Spa-Fields in Islington, the Enon Chapel in Clement's Lane, and the neighbouring oddly named 'Green Ground' in Portugal Street, now partly under the London School of Economics library. These grounds, used by the poorer classes, were not consecrated and the lack of solemnity and decorum associated with burials there became a matter of scandal, on which Chadwick felt compelled to comment:

On occasions of several interments taking place in burial-grounds in the metropolis at the same time, the master undertakers will volunteer their services to get the crowd of by-standers into some order, and show how much might be done by other and better superintendence to add to the impressiveness of the last scene. The inferior attendants, the grave-diggers, at the interments which I have witnessed at the new cemeteries, attended, as they usually do at the parochial grounds, in a disorderly condition – unshaven, dirty in person, in dirty shirts and in the old and the common filthy dress. During the burial service the undertakers' men only concerned themselves in removing the feathers from the hearse and preparing for an immediate return; all the attendants began talking on other matters, and went their different ways immediately the coffin was lowered; the mourners were left with the utmost unconcern, except by the grave-diggers, who followed them in the attitude of the usual solicitations of money for drink.

The practice of removing coffins almost

immediately after a burial, and chopping them up to make room for more corpses in an area of limited space was common. Often the coffins may have only lain in the ground for a matter of days or weeks. There were many London churchyards and private burial grounds where the remnants of coffins could be seen scattered around. Of these practices Knight comments that they

....have taken place at Enon Chapel, the Globe Fields, St Andrew's Undershaft, St Anne's, Soho (where the wonderful man Fox did not mind cutting through a body buried but three weeks), St Clement's churchyard, St Clement Danes, St Martin's in the Fields (Drury Lane), St Mary's, Vinegar Yard – in short, at so many places that it is far from improbable that the greater part of London grave-yards have witnessed similar scenes. Among the minor practices of the grave-yard gentry, may be mentioned the interring bodies at insufficient depth when they happened to be in an idle mood, and then, when it became necessary to turn the spot to the best advantage, of digging the coffins up, and re-burying them at the suitable depth. From a similar motive, when a deep grave has been dug, it appears that it is sometimes allowed to remain open till it is filled, boards and earth being merely placed over the top. At the grave-yard in Drury Lane they gradually waxed so confident in this habit, that even when the unhappy relatives said they did not like to go away without seeing the grave filled up, they pertinaciously refused.

The reports related to the above will be examined in more detail in chapter three.

Dickensian Gloom

Charles Dickens (1812-70) conveyed some of the atmosphere and squalor common to many London churchyards in the early to mid 19th century. Scenes from *Bleak House* are often quoted to convey their gloomy dankness.

At last we stood under a dark and miserable covered way, where one lamp was burning over an iron gate and where the morning faintly struggled in. The gate was closed. Beyond it was a burial ground – a dreadful spot in which the night was very slowly stirring, but where I could see heaps of dishonoured graves and stones, hemmed in by filthy houses with a few dull lights in their windows and on whose walls a thick humidity broke out like a disease.[7]

There have been attempts to locate some of the churchyards which Dickens described, but omitted to name. It is contended that the churchyard associated with the *Bleak House* character 'Poor Jo' is identified in a letter that Dickens wrote from Boston on 4 April 1868:

Convey yourself back to London by the agency of that powerful Locomotive, your imagination, and walk through the centre avenue of Covent Garden Market from West to East:- that is to say, with your back towards the church, and your face towards Drury Lane Theatre. Keep straight on along the side of the Theatre, and about halfway down, on the left side of the way, behind the houses, is a closely hemmed in grave yard – happily long disused and closed by the Law. I do not remember that the grave-yard is accessible from the street now, but when I was a boy it was to be got at by a low covered passage under a house, and was guarded by a rusty iron gate. In that churchyard I long afterwards buried the 'Nemo' of *Bleak House*.[8]

It was of this Drury Lane burial ground that George Walker in his *Gatherings from Grave Yards*, had written that:

....many thousands of bodies have been here deposited. The substratum was, some years since, so saturated with dead, that the place 'was shut up' for a period. The ground was subsequently raised to its present height – level with the first floor windows surrounding the place, and in this superstratum vast numbers of bodies have, up to this period, been deposited. A short time since a pit was dug (a very common practice here) in one corner of the ground; in it many bodies were deposited at different periods, the top of the pit being covered only with boards. This ground is a most intolerable and highly dangerous nuisance to the entire neighbourhood. Rather more than two years ago, in making three areas to the centre houses on the western side of this burying ground, many bodies were disturbed and mutilated; the inhabitants of the houses frequently annoyed by the most disgusting and repulsive sights.

Chadwick paints a black picture of the environment in the neighbourhood of churches we now associate as being in exclusive areas, with perhaps the exception of St Giles-in-the-Fields. He comments in his report:

In the parishes of St Giles-in-the-Fields, St George, Hanover Square, St James Westminster, and St Martin's-in-the-Fields, over-crowding of the burial grounds within the parish, between forty and fifty years ago, led the parish officers to obtain local acts for the establishment of burial grounds in the suburbs ...[9]

The situation described by Chadwick and Walker will be looked at in chapter three.

Early Burial Grounds

Londinium, the Roman city, still survives in many forms beneath the streets of London. Roman burials are frequently uncovered. A recent Museum of London report noted that Smithfield, St Bartholomew's Hospital, Newgate Street and Paternoster Row are sites of just a few newly uncovered burials.

Roman cemeteries were, by law, situated outside the town and evidence for Roman Londoners is found in the cemeteries sited along the main roads that led out of town, beyond the city gates of Aldgate, Bishopsgate, Aldersgate, Newgate and Ludgate on the landward side of the town, and south beyond the settlement in Southwark. Roman burial practices found in London are well paralleled elsewhere and bodies were either cremated or buried. In total we know of over 1100 burials from Roman London but many must also have gone unrecognised in the past. Excavations in recent years have revealed several extensive cemetery areas, including 80 burials at Spitalfields in the northern cemetery and 25 burials from Great Dover Street in the southern cemetery.[10]

St Paul's cathedral and the Tower of London have produced finds dating back to the Roman era. Early historians of London, in particular John Stow, have described the unearthing of Roman burials, pottery and coins. In 1576, while observing digging for clay at Spittle Field, Stow noted that:

On the east side of this churchyard lieth a large field, of old time called Lolesworth, now Spittle field; which about the year 1576 was broken up for clay to make brick; in the digging whereof many earthen pots, called urna, were found full of ashes, and burnt bones of men, to wit, of the Romans that inhabited here; for it was the custom of the Romans to burn their dead, to put their ashes in an urn, and then bury the same, with certain ceremonies, in some field appointed for that purpose near unto their city. Every one of these pots had in them with the ashes of the dead one piece of copper money, with the inscription of the emperor then reigning: some of them were of Claudius, some of Vespasian, some of Nero, of Anthoninus Pius, of Trajanus, and others.[11]

An excavation beween 1983 and 1990 near the former Spitalfields Market in east London, at the site of what was probably one of London's main Roman cemeteries, has yielded 672 inhumations and 134 cremations, forming the largest single sample of Roman burials in London, and one of the largest known in the country. Analysis has shown that they probably all belong to a single cemetery, the full extent of which cannot be estimated exactly, but could have contained well over 100,000 dead. This was in use from the first century AD to at least the end of the fourth century.[12]

Museum of London excavations 1998-1999 at Broadgate EC2 yielded seven Roman burials with grave goods which included bracelets and a coin. Also in 1999 another large excavation took place at Spitalfields Market in advance of the market's redevelopment. The site was that of the medieval priory and hospital of St Mary Spital of which nothing survives above ground. 8000 medieval burials were unearthed. Under these lay Roman skeletons which had been much damaged by centuries of development. Earlier work on the site had produced 19 Roman

6. The sarcophagus of 'Spitalfields Lady'.

skeletons and in the 1930s some Roman cremations were discovered. In 1999, 82 Roman skeletons were recovered from the ground including a sarcophagus containing the remains of a woman who was dubbed the 'Spitalfields Lady'.[13]

The development of Paternoster Square by St Paul's Cathedral yielded further Roman burials dating from the beginning of the Roman occupation through to the 4th century.[14]

In 2006 a Museum of London excavation in the vaults of St Martin-in-the-Fields, Trafalgar Square, produced a limestone coffin containing a headless body which was dated to the period 390 to 430 AD. Excavations carried out by the Museum over the last decade discovered an intact Roman coffin in Holborn in 2005 and in the same year a wooden Roman coffin was unearthed in Holborn during building work alongside the Fleet river. A Roman cemetery was discovered in 2002 on America Street in Southwark dating from between the 2nd-4th century. 166 burials were excavated some of which excited curiosity. One grave contained a man embracing a woman, with an infant lying between them suggesting that this was a family group who may have died within a very short time of each other. Another grave contained the skeleton of a man who had been buried with the head of an old horse, the probability being that it was a lifetime pet. Yet another grave contained the burial of a male adult with bound legs, and a spear point stabbed through both ankles. Yet another skeleton was found with a coin in its mouth, which would

7. Spitalfields burial pit under the charnel house.

have been the payment for Charon, the ferryman once the deceased reached the the River Styx.[15]

Probably the most dramatic, and poignant periods of London burials are those that date from the 1348/9 Black Death, and the Great Plague of 1665. This period is dealt with in the following chapter.

1 Charles Knight, *London*, (1841, 1851 edn), vol. 3, p.168.
2 *Ibid*, p.166.
3 Edwin Chadwick, *A report on the results of a special inquiry into the practice of interment in towns, etc*, (1845) ed. by C Sherman, p.134.
4 *ibid* p.137.
5 *ibid* p.138.
6 *ibid* p.140.
7 Charles Dickens, *Bleak House*, Ch. 14.
8 Trevor Blount. 'The Graveyard Satire of *Bleak House* in the Context of 1850' in *The Review of English Studies*, New Series, vol. 14, No. 56. (Nov. 1963), p. 370.
9 Chadwick, pp 97-8.
10 http://www.classicalassociation.org/extracts/JHall.htm.extracts/JHall.htm.
11 John Stow, *Survey of London* (1598, 1840 edn.), p.64.
12 http://www.eng-h.gov.uk/archrev/rev94_5/eastcem.htm
13 See for a more detailed report: http://www.britarch.ac.uk/ba/ba50/ba50feat.html
14 For more information see http://www.molas.org.ukpagessiteReports.asp?siteid=ngt00&section=preface
15 http://www.britarch.ac.uk/BA/ba67/news.shtml#item4

CHAPTER TWO

PLAGUE PITS AND PEST FIELDS

Legacy of the Black Death and Great Plague

The so-called Black Death of 1348/9 was bubonic plague, one of three types of plague. It is caused by the bacterium *yersinia pestis* existing in the bloodstream of rodents, in this case, probably rats. It is believed that fleas, having sucked the blood of the rats, then transferred the disease to humans by bites, though also by the infected faeces of fleas entering the skin via lesions etc. The symptoms are that the lymph system becomes inflamed showing dark swollen areas where there are lymph nodes. A plague which is 'pneumonic' occurs when the same bacterium infects the lungs: any airborne particle from the breath of the infected person can infect another person who inhales the particles.

The Black Death, that was to ravish London and most of Europe, originated in China and carved its deadly course to London by way of trade. Estimates of the percentage that succumbed in 1348/9 vary from a third of London's population to nearly a half.

It was under these circumstances that the need to undertake mass burials led to a proliferation of extra burial grounds. The Black Death and Great Plague of 1665 have created their own brand of London burial mythology. Scarcely do workmen strike disordered or scattered human remains, not an uncommon occurrence in central London, than there is a presumption that the site must be a 'plague pit'. Unsubstantiated tales of plague pits are used to

8. A remnant of Knightsbridge Green in 2008. It was described by Holmes in 1896 as a burial ground for 'victims of the plague from the leper hospital ... A grassy, closed triangle copposite Tattersall's.' The Tattersall's Tavern back left is a reminder.

explain patches of land in prime areas not built upon, such as Knightsbridge Green. There is an increasingly popular genre of 'ghosts of the London underground' many of which are associated with the disturbance of the dead during construction of underground and railway tunnels. Vanessa Harding, an authority on such burials, comments that 'the site of any discovery of plentiful human remains in a location no longer used for burial tends to be identified as a plague pit, unless a more reliable history is quickly attached to it. There were undoubtedly some temporary and irregular plague burial sites, but though few are well documented, their overall number may have been quite limited.'[1] Church records often refer to plague burials in their churchyards, and some contemporary witnesses, such as Pepys, Evelyn, and Defoe, give us an idea of where to look for these sites. Many burial pits were indeed in churchyards, and in some grounds, such as at Stepney, where the plague burial area is now railed off for dog walking (see chapter three), the pit area can still be identified.

Plague is first recorded in London in 664, returning at intervals until the latter part of the 17th century. On its arrival in 1348/9 London's churchyards already provided too little space for the numbers that needed burying. Smithfield and Charterhouse were sites designated to receive many of the plague victims. As for the number of Londoners who perished, a stone cross of the time at Charterhouse claimed 'more than fifty thousand' were buried there alone. But this seems exaggerated.[2] Stow's *Survey of London,* published first in 1598, tells us:

And without the bar of West Smithfield lieth a large street or way, called of the house of St John there St John's Street ... A great pestilence entering this island ... so wasting the people that scarce the tenth person of all sorts was left alive, and churchyards were not sufficient to receive the dead, but men were forced to choose out certain fields for burials; whereupon Ralph Stratford, Bishop of London, in the year 1348, bought a piece of ground called No Man's Land, where he enclosed with a wall of brick, and dedicated for burial of the dead, building thereupon a proper chapel, which is now enlarged and made a dwelling-house; and this burying-plot is become a fair garden, retaining the old nave of Pardon Churchyard ... in the year 1349 ... Sir Walter Manny, in respect of danger that might befall in this time of so great a plague and infection, purchased thirteen acres and a rod of ground adjoining the said No Man's Land, and lying in a place called Spittle Cross, because it belonged to St. Bartholomew's Hospital, since that called the New Church Haw, and caused it to be consecrated by the said bishop of London to the use of burials ... In this plot of ground there were in that year more than fifty thousand persons buried ... it is to be noted that above one hundred thousand bodies of Christian people had in that churchyard been buried; for the said knight had purchased that place for the burial of poor people, travellers, and others that were deceased, to remain for ever.[3]

The historian John Noorthouck (1732-1816), writing in 1773, adds that this area:

... was long remembered by an inscription fixed on a stone cross upon the premises. On this burial ground the Charter-House now stands. There was also another piece of ground purchased at the east end of the city, just without the wall, by one John Corey, a clergyman, for the same use; on which spot was afterward, in this same reign, founded the abbey of St Mary of Grace, for Cistertian monks: it is now covered by the victualling-office, and adjoining houses. It was asserted that not one in ten escaped this calamity; and that not less than 100,000 persons died in the whole.[4]

The Plague of 1665 severely taxed London's infrastructure – about 100,000 Londoners perished. Exact figures are impossible to determine as many burials were not recorded. 'Dead-wagons' collected the deceased at night, conveying them to burial pits which remained open until full. Daniel Defoe's account of the period, *Journal of the Plague Year* (1722), is frequently alluded to by historians and it does have an aura of immediacy and authority. However, Defoe (*c.* 1660-1731) was a child at the time of the Plague and his sources are not known. What Defoe does however

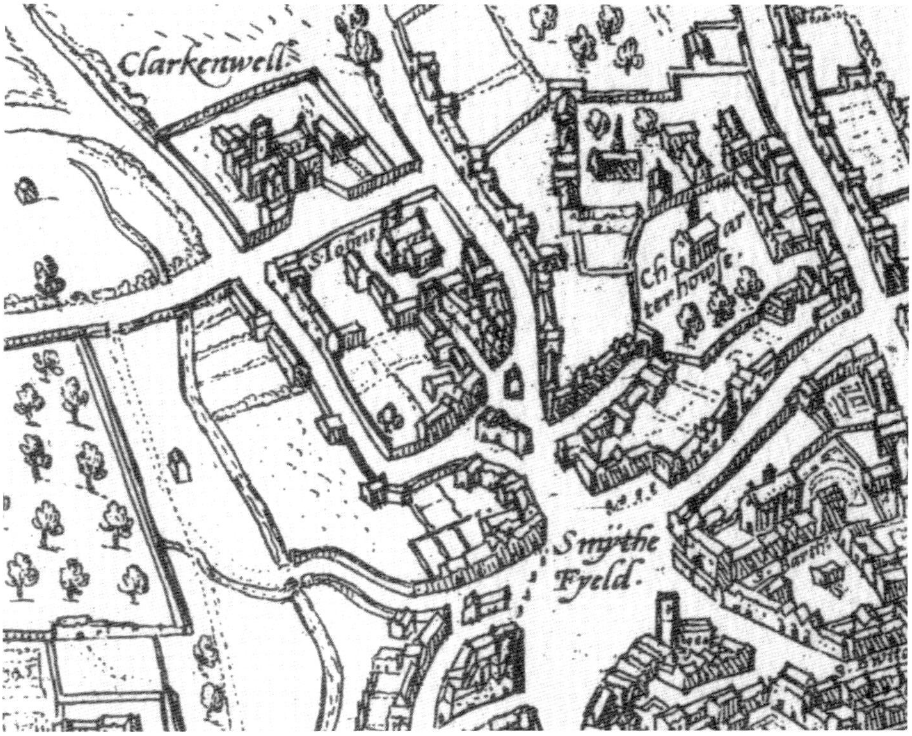

9. *Braun & Hogenberg's map of 1572 showing Smithfield, St John's off Clerkenwell, and to the right, Charterhouse Square, the site of numerous burials.*

is name sites where pits were dug and the dead hurriedly interred.

Charterhouse

The London Charterhouse was founded by Sir Walter Manny in 1371. It was situated immediately outside the city walls, close to Smithfield Market and thrived as a monastic institution until its suppression in 1538. Three burial grounds were created there as the London churchyards began to fill. The one to the north was known originally as 'Nomannesland' and was founded in 1348 by the Bishop of London, Ralph de Stratford. It was later known as the Pardon Churchyard (not to be confused with that near St Paul's). Stow commented that at the time of his writing it 'served for burying of such as desperately ended their lives, or were executed for felonies, who were fetched thither usually in a close cart ...'[5] It is probable that this ground was situated between Great Sutton Street, and the south side of today's Clerkenwell Road. The cemetery to the south which covers a large part of Charterhouse Square was founded shortly afterwards, either at the end of 1348 or beginning of 1349. This lay within the area 'Spitalcroft', in land leased from St Bartholomew's Hospital.[6] A Museum of London volume on Charterhouse (*London Charterhouse*, MoLAS 2002) estimates that in these combined (West) Smithfield cemeteries, based on numbers at *East* Smithfield near Tower Hill, another Black Death burial ground, there are around 10,000 bodies.

Commenting on these three grounds, Mrs. Holmes, wrote that Pardon Churchyard was located at:

Wilderness Row, now merged into Clerkenwell Road ... while the gardens and courts of the Charterhouse, the Square, the site of a demolished burial-ground for

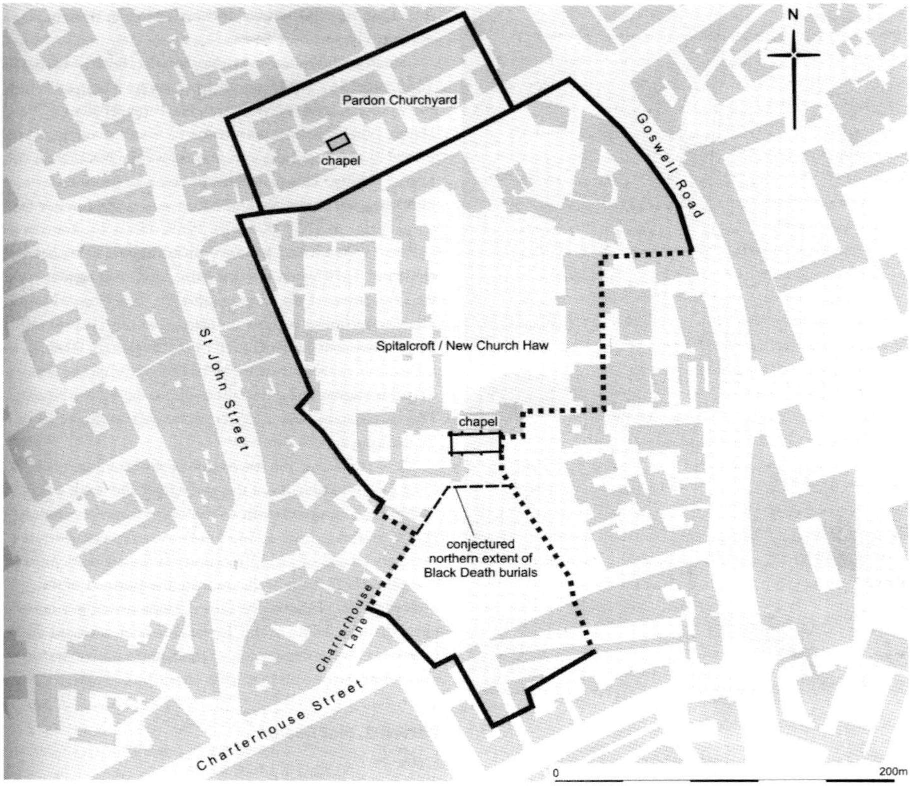

10. Diagram of two of the Charterhouse burial grounds. The Black Death burials to the south cover much of the present-day Charterhouse Square. (From The London Charterhouse, MoLAS Monograph 10).

the pensioners (Sutton's Ground), and the burial-ground which still exists at the northern end of the precincts, are all part of the Spittle Croft and of the monastery burial ground ... the 'Victualling-office', [for the Charterhouse] which took the place of St Mary's Abbey, was where the Royal Mint at present stands, and ... the abbey graveyard was where the entrance courtyard is now.[7]

An article in *Notes and Queries* of 2 July1853 noted that: 'When the ground in Charterhouse Square was opened in 1834, for the purposes of sewerage (I believe), vast numbers of bones and skeletons were found, being the remains, as was supposed, of those who died of the Plague in 1348, and had been interred in that spot, as forming a part of Pardon Churchyard, which had lately been purchased by Sir Walter Manny, for the purposes of burial, and attached to the Carthusian convent there.'

And when in March 2000 some disarticulated human bones were found on the site of Nos. 35-42 Clerkenwell Road, the Museum of London stated that this was 'the first archaeological evidence of the location of the Pardon churchyard and indicates that any future development in the vicinity of this site should be subject to detailed archaeological assessment prior to any work commencing.'[18]

Echoes of the 1665 Plague

The impact of the Great Plague was such that evidence of mass burials can still be seen over 350 years later.

When deaths became so numerous, the church-yards

11. *Charterhouse Square in 2008. 'When the ground was opened in 1834 for the purposes of sewerage ... vast numbers of bones and skeletons were found.'*

were unable to contain the bodies, and the usual modes of interment were no longer observed: occasional pits of great capacity were dug in several parts, to which the dead were brought by cartloads, collected by the ring of a bell, and the doleful cry of Bring out your dead! They were put into the carts with no other covering than rugs or sheets tied round them by their friends, if they had any surviving; and were shot down in promiscuous heaps! Sometimes the drivers of these carts would drop in their employments, and the carts would be found without any conductor; in the parish of Stepney it was said they lost within the year,116 sextons, grave-diggers, and their assistants![9]

Noorthouck observed that under the orders of the Earl of Craven and other justices of Westminster, 'the churchyards [were] covered two feet thick with fresh earth; to prevent as far as possible any revival of the pestilential taint.'[10] Such was the fear of contracting the disease that he states,

It was well known that numbers of poor despairing creatures wandered out of town into the fields, woods and other remote places, where they died of the infection and of want. The inhabitants of the villages would carry food to these distracted refugees and set it at a distance for them; and frequently found them dead afterward with the victuals untouched. The country people would then dig holes and drag the bodies into them with long poles having hooks at the ends, carefully standing to the windward; and throw the earth over them as far as they could cast it.[11]

Holmes commented that 'it is pretty certain that many unrecorded burials took place in the fields of Stoke Newington.

Some London Plague burials 1665

Defoe mentions a number of pits, churchyards and burial grounds where victims of the 1665 plague were interred. Some references identify the location, some are only vague. One in the vicinity of Petticoat Lane has never been located. Defoe wrote:

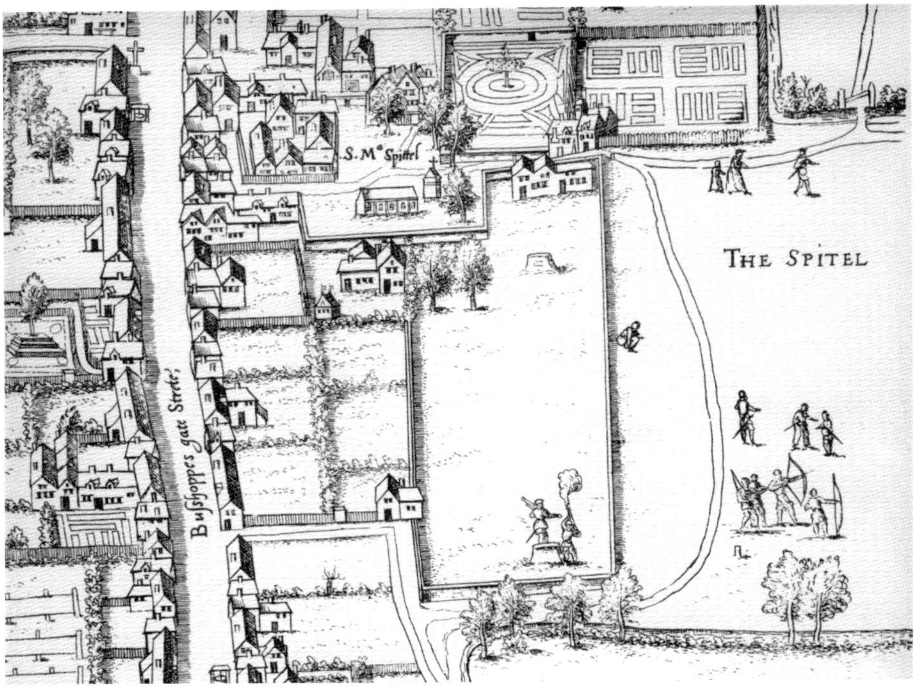

12 & 13. *Spitalfields, mentioned by Defoe (number 5 on p. 24) as having two plague burial sites. Above is a section from the 'Agas' map of c. 1562 showing the rural nature of Spitalfields in the 16th century. The buildings shown in mid-left section approximate to modern day Liverpool Street. Below is an illustration of the extensive nature of the Spitalfields Market excavations between 1997 and 1998.*

14. A burial pit at Spitalfields underneath a charnel house.

The distemper sweeping away such multitudes as I have observed, many, if not all the out-parishes were obliged to make new burying-grounds, besides that I have mentioned in Bunhill Fields, some of which were continued, and remain in use to this day.[12]

Defoe continues:

But others were left off, and which, I confess, I mention with some reflection, being converted into other uses or built upon afterwards, the dead bodies were disturbed, abused, dug up again, some even before the flesh of them was perished from the bones, and removed like dung or rubbish to other places.

Defoe then identifies those sites that 'came within reach of [his] observation'.

He numbers them:

1. A piece of ground beyond Goswell Street, near Mount Mill, being some of the remains of the old lines of fortifications of the city, where abundance were buried promiscuously from the parishes of Aldersgate, Clerkenwell, and even out of the city. This ground, as I take it, was since made a physic garden, and after that it has been built upon.

2. A piece of ground just over the Black Ditch, as it was then called, at the end of Holloway Lane, in Shoreditch parish. It has been since made a yard for keeping hogs, and for other ordinary uses, but is quite out of use as a burying-ground.

3. The upper end of Hand Alley, in Bishopsgate Street, which was then a green field, and was taken in particularly for Bishopsgate parish, though many of the carts out of the city brought their dead thither also, particularly out of the parish of St Allhallows on the Wall.

It is likely that the upper end of Hand Alley is the present-day site of Cutlers' Gardens. The Ogilby & Morgan map of 1676 shows the ground today occupied by Devonshire Square to be open in the correct location and Holmes tells us that New Street and Bishopsgate Street occupy the site of the former Hand Alley.

Defoe takes the opportunity to settle a score with a former, safely deceased enemy, Sir Robert Clayton:

'This place [Hand Alley] I cannot mention without much regret. It was, as I remember, about two or three years after the plague was ceased that Sir Robert Clayton came to be possessed of the ground. It was reported, how true I know not, that it fell to the king for want of heirs, all those who had any right to it being carried off by the pestilence, and that Sir Robert Clayton obtained a grant of it from King Charles II. But however he came by it, certain it is, the ground was let out to build on, or built upon by his order: the first house built upon it was a large fair house still standing, which faces the street, or way, now called Hand-Alley, which though called an alley, is as wide as a street: the houses in the same row with that house northward, are built on the very same ground where the poor people are buried, and the bodies on opening the ground for the foundation, were dug up, some of them remaining so plain to be seen, that the women's skulls were distinguished by their long hair, and of others, the flesh was not quite perished; so that the people began to exclaim loudly against it, and some suggested that it might endanger a return of the contagion: after which the bones and bodies as fast as they came at them, were carried to another part of the same ground, and thrown altogether into a deep pit, dug on purpose, which now is to be known, in that it is not built on, but is a passage to another house, at the upper end of Rose Alley, just against the door of a Meeting-House, which has been there many years since; and the ground is palisadoed off from the rest of the passage, in a little square; there lies the bones and remains of near two thousand bodies, carried by the dead carts to their grave in that one year.

Defoe continues:

4. Besides this, there was a piece of Ground in Moorfields, by the going into the street, which is now called Old Bethlem, which was enlarged, much, though not wholly taken in on the same Occasion.

5. Stepney Parish extending itself from the East part of London to the North, even to the very edge of Shoreditch Churchyard to the north, even to the very edge of Shoreditch Churchyard, had a piece of ground taken in to bury their dead close to the said churchyard, and which for that very reason was left open, and is since, I suppose, taken into the same churchyard. And they had also two other burying-places in Spitalfields, one where since a chapel or tabernacle has been built for ease to this great parish, and another in Petticoat Lane.

Defoe then informs us that,

There were no less than five other grounds made use of for the parish of Stepney at that time, one where now stands the parish church of St Paul, Shadwell, and the other where now stands the parish church of St John's at Wapping, both which had not the names of parishes at that time, but were belonging to Stepney parish.[13]

Each of Defoe's five grounds will be looked at individually. Holmes attempted to identify those not specifically delineated. Of the 'Black Ditch' (2) mentioned by Defoe, Holmes believes this to be 'Holywell Mount' (see illustration 19) which

15. Cloisters in the north walk at Westminster Abbey. A plaque records that 26 monks perished from the Black Death and were buried in a single grave.

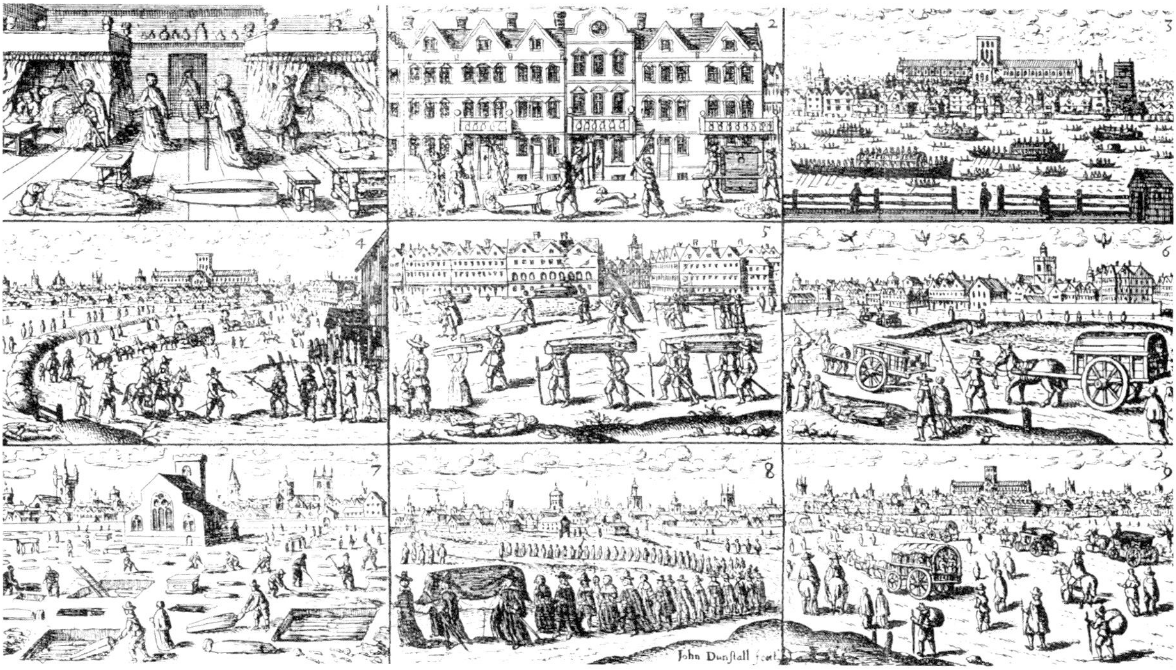

16. A pictorial broadside of 1665, depicting scenes from the Great Plague.

17. Hand Alley – was Cutlers' Gardens, now Devonshire Square – is the location of one of Defoe's plague burial sites.

18. (Top) Bunhill Fields in 2008. A possible burial ground for plague victims.

19. (Above) The site of Holywell Mount, one of Defoe's plague pits, beneath the site of the present 21 Curtain Road.

20. (Right) View of plague victims being buried at Holywell Lane, Shoreditch, in 1665.

was used as a plague pit both prior to 1665 and for burials after the plague. It was named after the neighbouring Holywell Convent. At the end of the 1890s there was a small section of the ground remaining, approximately a quarter of an acre. 'It is behind the church of St James', Curtain Road, and is approached by a passage from Holywell Row. A parish room has been built on it, and what remains is used as a timber yard. The piece between the parish room and the church is bare and untidy.'[14] The burial area is located where 21 Curtain Road now stands. The area of Defoe's plague pit is still an open yard visible from 38 Scrutton Street, in Finsbury, EC2.

Liverpool Street Station and Broadgate, EC2 (Bethlem or New Ground)

This site was used during periods of plague, and at other times by parishes with limited burial space. It continued in use until around 1720. It first disappeared under the Broad Street station booking office (opened 1865) and now lies beneath the Broadgate development.

The greater part of the burden of accommodating the plague dead fell on the parishes. However, there were two important civic initiatives in this period which helped to relieve pressure on burial space without resort to irregular practices. The first was the opening of the New Churchyard at Bethlem in 1569. Until then London had had no significant extra-parochial burial ground, though St Paul's churchyard in the city centre had always been a popular burial site, especially with inhabitants of the small parishes around the cathedral. Some of the dead in the plague of 1563 were buried there, and the number of deaths in this epidemic spurred the Mayor and aldermen to action: in 1569, believing that space in the churchyards of the City might be insufficient if such an epidemic happened again, they established a new burial ground 'before the time of necessity requireth it'. The City used a site of about one acre already belonging to it, adjoining the north-east side of Moorfields, part of the lands of Bethlem Hospital.

The plot, until then used as a tenterground, was walled in at the expense of Sir Thomas Rowe, then Lord Mayor, usually credited as the

21. Rocque's map of c. 1746 shows the churchyard on the corner of Wormwood Street and Bishopsgate where Liverpool Street station now stands. The Bethlem Burying Ground to the north-west lies under the Broadgate development.

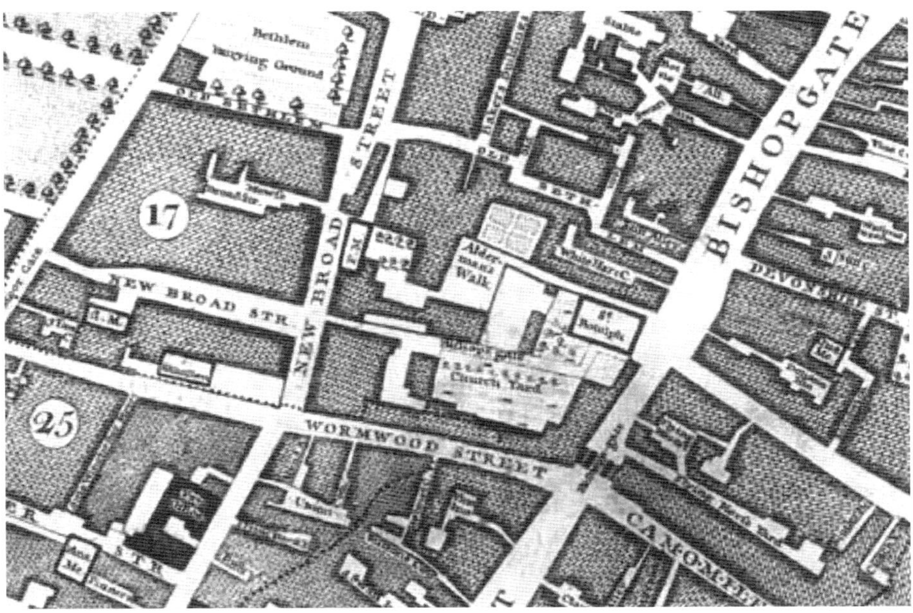

22. View from Camomile Street, itself the site of a burial ground, looking towards Liverpool Street station on the left, also on the site of a burial ground, as is Broadgate on the right.

New Churchyard's founder. Though the immediate incentive was the fear of an excessive number of plague dead, and the new ground was certainly used for many burials in later epidemics, it was also used extensively in non-plague years by a number of parishes with limited local accommodation, and remained in use until around 1720.

The hospital derived its name from the Priory of St Mary Bethlehem, founded there in 1247. From 1377 the hospital began to specialise in looking after 'distracted' patients. In the 1670s the hospital moved to Moorfields, by which time the behaviour of patients was a source of perverted entertainment on viewing days.

The old burial ground came to light again in 2004 when a trench for electrical cables was dug between Finsbury Market and Bishopsgate which ran through the western end of Liverpool Street. A large number of bones and two complete skeletons were uncovered which 'almost certainly derive from the Bethlem Church Ground'.[15]

Holmes noted that 'the Churchyard and the Asylum have disappeared, Liverpool Street Station having taken their place, and hundreds of the Great Eastern Railway goods vans daily roll over the mouldering remains of the departed citizens.'[16] Part of the site was excavated in 1986 and burials were found to be very dense. A brick vault was found, containing members of the Jenks family in lead coffins, dated 1686 -1714.[17]

23. Bethlem Hospital, rebuilt here in Moorfields in the mid 1670s.

24. *St Paul's Shadwell, a Stepney church whose churchyard was used for plague burials in 1665.*

St Paul's church, The Highway, Shadwell, E1

Of the five grounds specified by Defoe as plague burial sites for the parish of Stepney, two are the grounds of the parish churches of St Paul's Shadwell and St John at Wapping.

The original St Paul's Shadwell, erected in 1656, was a Stepney chapel-of-ease and was rebuilt as the parish church of Shadwell in 1669. The existing building, designed by John Walters, dates from 1820. The churchyard is a little under an acre and is neat and well maintained. There is nothing, despite Defoe's assertion, to indicate the site of the plague pit. Walker commented in 1839 that 'the ground adjoining the church is very full, and so also are the vaults underneath it.'[18]

By the end of that century Holmes was able to comment that the churchyard, which was laid out as gardens in 1886, was 'now maintained and kept in good order...'

St John's church, Wapping, Green Bank, E1
Additional ground opposite

This church and its environs are worth a visit. The school next to the church has now been converted into private apartments, but the area of the church and churchyard retains the atmosphere of an earlier age. The ground is extensive, but the section which contains the site of the plague pit is the additional ground, entered by a gate directly opposite the church entrance. Holmes describes it as being 'rather over ½ acre. This was one of the Stepney pest-fields. It is closed, but tidy. There are quantities of tombstones in this ground, many of which seem to be falling to pieces, and an unusual number of trees and flowering shrubs.'

25. The burial ground of St John at Wapping, used for 1665 plague burials.

26. St John Additional ground, site of a plague pit. The school building on the right was dedicated in 1760 and probably built over a part of the original ground.

Whitechapel

Three further Defoe plague burial sites were looked for by Holmes. She comments that 'one was possibly in Gower's Walk, Whitechapel, where human remains, without coffins were come upon recently in digging the foundation for Messrs. Kinloch's new buildings. The remains were moved in boxes to a railway arch in Battersea in the winter of 1893-4.'[19]

Some sites in this area are not mentioned by Defoe, such as a ground on the north side of Mile End Road in Whitechapel. In 1896, according to Holmes, the site was 'occupied by houses south of the junction of Lisbon and Collingwood Streets, Cambridge Road.' Another such area lies near the London Hospital in Whitechapel Road. Holmes writes '... it is certain that a large tract of land south of the London Hospital was

27. (Left) Gower's Walk in 2008. Probably another of Defoe's plague pits. Mrs Holmes witnessed bones being removed from here. The site is being redeveloped at the time of writing.

28 St Philip's church, adjoining the London Hospital, covers a 1665 plague pit.

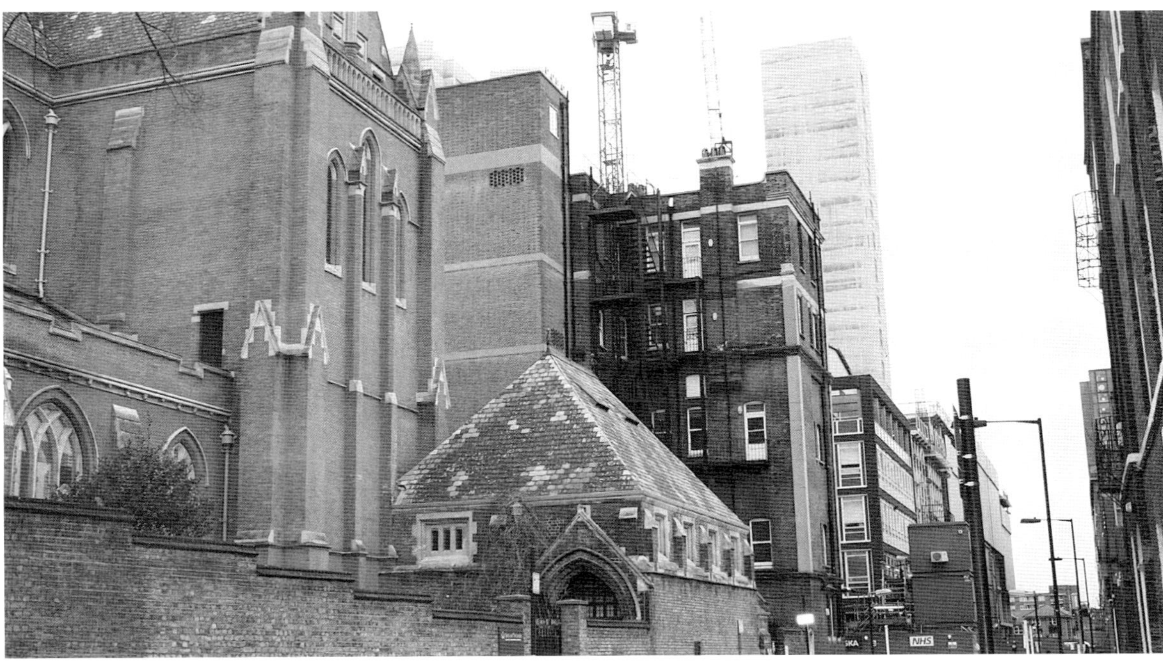

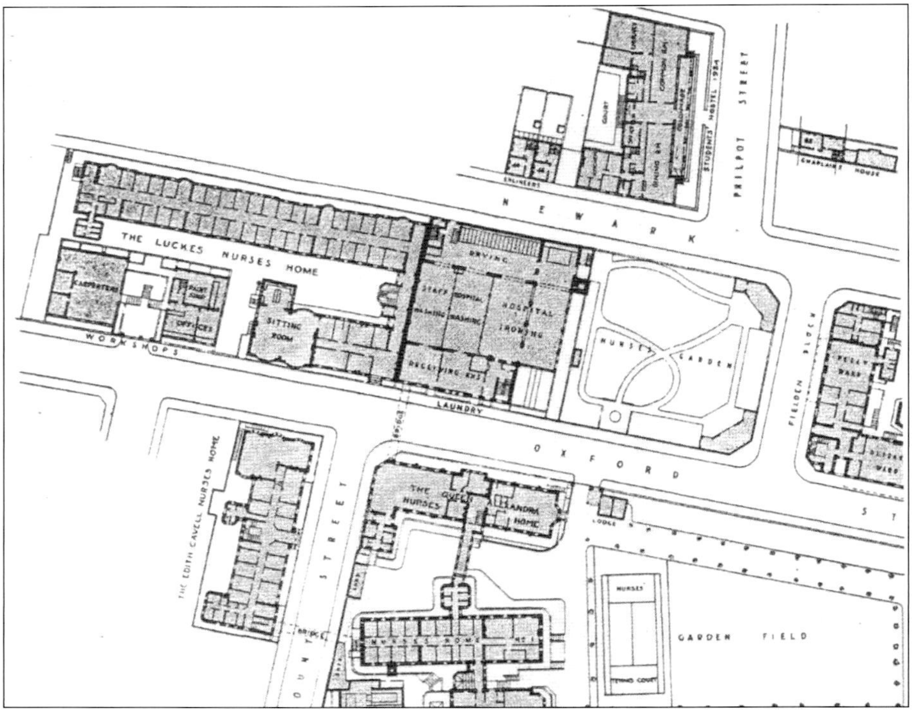

29. London Hospital courtyard. Much of the area around and to the immediate south of the hospital was the site of a burial ground. The nurses' tennis court sometimes subsided when coffins beneath it gave way. The court can be seen bottom centre right.

30. The London Hospital burial ground. Note the position of the steeple of St Philip's church peeping up on the far side – a photograph published in Mrs Holmes' book. Much of the foreground was a burial ground.

also used for interments, and the Brewer's Garden and the site of St Philip's Church were probably parts of this ground, which was known as Stepney Mount.'[20] Brewer's Gardens were a short distance along the street from St Philip's church.

Holmes also describes a large area immediately south of the hospital as being a burial ground. She writes that

> ... the 'unclaimed corpses' from the London Hospital found their last resting-place very near home. In 1849 the whole of the southern part of the enclosure, quite an acre and a half, was the burial ground, and here, although it was closed by order in Council in 1854, it appears that burials took place until about 1860, one of the present porters remembering his father acting as a gravedigger. The medical school, the chaplain's house, and the nurses' home have all been built upon it, and it is sincerely to be hoped that no further encroachments will be permitted. The remaining part

is the nurses' and students' garden and tennis-court, where they are in the habit of capering about in their short times off duty, and where it sometimes happens that the grass gives way beneath them – an ordinary occurrence when the subsoil is inhabited by coffins![21]

In 2003 when the Museum of London carried out a watching brief at the Tennis Court site, two test pits were dug with the expectation of finding human remains, but without success. Its report states that 'It is possible that human remains associated with post-medieval burial grounds may still be present at a lower level than that reached by either of these test pits.'[22]

St Bride's Churchyard, Fleet Street EC4

This churchyard is interesting for a number of reasons, not least that the nearby crypt once contained the remains of the novelist Samuel Richardson (1689-1761), whose coffin was discovered in 1993 during archaeological work. An article on the discovery and pathology of

31. St Bride's church and churchyard, early 19th century.

32. St Bride's churchyard today. Note the height of the ground against the surrounding buildings, the result of large numbers of burials.

33. *An iron coffin on display in the crypt of St Bride's. It was devised to foil body snatchers, but in 1820, following a court judgment, such coffins were banned because they took much longer to disintegrate than wooden coffins – and burial space was scarce.*

Richardson's remains appears in *Current Archaeology* issue 190 (February 2004). The crypt has now been transformed into a museum, arranged with well preserved tombstones, and an iron coffin. The churchyard was used extensively during the 1665 plague as was the nearby St Dunstan's. Vanessa Harding comments that:

The records of St Bride's also show that at least two of the expedients often considered characteristic of plague burial in London, the organized collection of corpses and the opening of mass graves, were at least to begin with parish initiatives. St Bride's and St Dunstan's jointly employed a party of bearers from July onwards; an early reference to 'slinges to carry the dead corpes', and the absence of any later references to carts suggests that bearing was always done on foot in these parishes. Other parishes, perhaps especially the larger ones, bought or hired carts as they found necessary. It is difficult to discover whether a centralized system of dead-carts ever existed, or whether it was always carried out by parishes, perhaps acting together in groups. Defoe says that "the dead carts in the city were not confined to particular parishes, but one cart went through several parishes, according as the number of dead presented," but, if this is so, the means by which this was organized and financed is not clear.[23]

The cost of dealing with the plague did become an issue, as Vanessa Harding describes:

In the 1665 plaque, at St Dunstan in the West, the first pits were dug in mid-August; at St Bride's, as we have seen, in late August. At St Botolph Aldgate a number of pits were dug in August, but the 'great pit' in the churchyard, and which came to contain over a thousand bodies, received its first corpse on 6 September, according to Defoe's account. 'Some blamed the churchwardens for suffering such a frightful thing ... but time made it appear the churchwardens knew the condition of the parish better than they did': within a fortnight it had been filled up with 1,114 bodies. It seems likely that most, perhaps all, of the larger suburban parishes of London ended by burying their

34. Part of the crypt of St Bride's. Much has been turned into a museum.

plague dead in mass graves, but that the smaller city-centre parishes did not need to do so. The main motive for digging mass graves was obviously to accommodate the maximum number of corpses in a small space, but the parishes may also have been driven to it to save money. They were shouldering the massive financial burden of supporting 'visited' families, watching houses, searching and reporting the dead, and by the height of the epidemic the great majority of families could make no contribution to the cost of burial.[24]

About half way through 1665 plague victims were refused burial at St Bride's. Once the plague had ceased, St Bride's levelled its lower and middle churchyards. The existing churchyard is still extremely high above pavement level.

St Bride's Additional ground, Harp Alley

It is probable that at least part of the additional ground to St Bride's lies under a courtyard in the present Harp Alley. It is a small alley, easy to miss, situated alongside a large taxi rank. In 1991-2 excavations under 72-82 Farringdon

35. St Bride's Additional burial ground was west of today's Farringdon Street (shown on the Rocque's 1746 map as the location of Fleet Market). A courtyard in Harp Alley today probably lies above early burials.

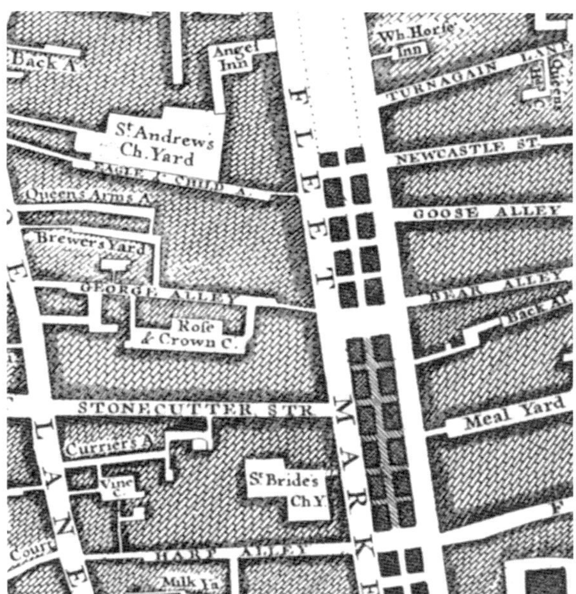

36. Westminster School scholars skating on ice near the pest houses on Tothill Fields.

37. Westminster School playing fields in Vincent Square, 2008. Here, according to Pepys, '1,200 Scotch prisoners, taken at the battle of Worcester' were interred.

Street produced 606 burials, 8 deep, and a brick burial vault.[25] Holmes notes that the ground 'off Farringdon Street, is about 750 square yards in extent, and used as a volunteer drill-ground. There are no tombstones, and the ground is untidy. Consecrated 1610. Given by the Earl of Dorset.'

Tothill Fields, Vincent Square, SW1

The area that is now the playing fields of Westminster School in Vincent Square, is part of the old Tothill Fields, as it still was in the time of Holmes. She describes it as comprising 8 acres in which 'some buildings have been erected.' She comments that 'A stone-paved yard in Earl Street is said to be the site of the plague pits, now the yard of Her Majesty's Stationery Office, Waste Paper Department.'

This would place the plague pits beneath Marsham Street between Horseferry Road and Vincent Street. Earl Street is now that part of Marsham Street. The area of the playing fields probably contained the remains of those who perished in the pest-houses. There is little to see now except for the playing fields themselves, to which access is restricted.

Here, too, were built the 'Five Houses', or 'Seven Chimneys', as pest-houses for plague victims, and in 1665 many were buried here. For 18 July, 1665, Samuel Pepys writes in his *Diary*: 'I was much troubled this day to hear at Westminster how the officers do bury the dead in the open Tuttle Fields, pretending want of room elsewhere; whereas the New Chapel churchyard was walled in at the publick charge in the last plague-time, merely for want of room, and now none but such as are able to pay dear for it can be buried there.' Here at Tothill, a short while previously, a substantial number of the 1,200 Scottish prisoners, taken at the Battle of Worcester (1651), were interred after execution; for in the accounts of the churchwardens of St Margaret's, Westminster, there is a payment of 'thirty shillings for sixty-seven loads of soil laid on the graves of Tothill Fields, wherein', it is added, 'the Scotch prisoners are buried'. Some of the Scots were 'driven like a herd of swine', says Heath's *Chronicle*, 'through Westminster to Tuthill Fields, and there sold to several merchants, and sent to the island of Barbadoes.'

The 'Five Houses', if we may trust *The Builder*, retained much of their primitive appearance in 1832. 'With the moss and lichens growing on the roofs and walls, and their generally old-fashioned quaintness, a very small stretch of the imagination removed the buildings which had surrounded them even then, and brought them once more into the open ground. They marked the site of a battery and breastwork when the fortifications around the cities of London and Westminster were hurriedly thrown up in 1642, by an order of Parliament. This battery is marked as about midway between the Chelsea Road and the bank of the river opposite Vauxhall.'[26]

Lillie Road Pest Field, Fulham

Distant from the plague burial grounds mentioned by Defoe, is one mentioned by Holmes in 1896, which was in Fulham and referred to as the Lillie Road Pest Field. Holmes writes:

Lillie Road Pest Field (the orchard of Normand House). – The site of this orchard, then 4 acres in extent, was used extensively for burials at the time of the Great Plague, Lintaine Grove now occupies part of it, and a row of houses in Lillie Road. Only about ¾ of an acre is still

38. Lillie Road Mansions on the corner of Tilton Street. Lillie Road Pest Field (at one time the orchard of Normand House), was used extensively for burials during the Great Plague of 1665.

39. The site of the Fulham Pools, and much of Normand Park, is a former plague and pest house burial ground.

unbuilt upon, at the corner of Tilton Street, and this is offered for sale.[27]

Part of this site is now being developed as Normand Park and Fulham Pools swimming baths now covers another section. On the ¾ of an acre, unbuilt on when Holmes wrote, is now Lillie Road Mansions.

Finsbury

Defoe mentions 'the great pit in Finsbury' as being a place of plague interments. This led to a commonly held belief that he was talking about Bunhill Fields cemetery. However, Walter Thornbury in his *Old and New London* (*c.* 1873) points out that Defoe was much more explicit about the site:

> The precise locality of Defoe's 'Pit' can be pointed out by any person familiar with the novelist's 'Journal' and the map of London. In the passage of Defoe which describes how John Hayward, the driver of a dead-cart, was on the point of consigning to the gloomy pit a wretched street-musician, who, whilst in a sound sleep, or perhaps stupefied with drink, had been thrown upon a load of corpses, the writer of the 'Journal', says, "Accordingly when John Hayward, with his bell and the cart, came along, finding two dead bodies lie upon the stall, they took them up with the instrument they used and threw them into the cart, and all this while the piper slept soundly. From thence they passed along and took in other dead bodies, till, as honest John Hayward told me, they almost buried him alive in the cart. Yet all this while he slept soundly. At length the cart came to the place where the bodies were to be thrown into the ground; which, as I do remember, was at Mountmill; and as the cart usually stopped some time before they were ready to shoot out the melancholy load they had in it—as soon as the cart stopped the fellow awaked, and struggled a little to get his head out from among the dead bodies; when, raising himself up in the cart, he called out, 'Hey! where am I?'[28]

The area of the Mount Mills pit sits slightly back from Goswell Road on the corner of Seward

40. Mount Mills on the corner of Seward Street; behind Goswell Road is the site of one of Defoe's plague pits.

41. The Mount Mills plague pit area.

42. Bunhill Fields burial ground c. 1920.

Street and Mount Mill. It is a narrow atmospheric residential area which is also host to a lost burial ground, barely 300 yards distant in Seward Street itself. The plague pit site is now partly a car park and partly a residential garden.

Bunhill Fields burial ground, City Road, EC1
Maitland in his *Survey of London* (1739) comments that 'Part of Bunhill Fields, at present denominated Tindal's, or the Dissenters' great Burial Ground, was, by the Mayor and Citizens of London, in the year 1665, set apart and consecrated as a common cemetery, for the interment of such corpses as could not have room in their own parochial burial-grounds in that dreadful year of pestilence. However, it not being made use of on that occasion, the said Tindal took a lease thereof, and converted it into a burial-ground for the use of Dissenters.' Two earlier sources, Strype in 1720, and Defoe in 1722 state otherwise, and it seems unlikely that at a time where burial land was in such urgent need, that it wouldn't have been used for this purpose. As Vanessa Harding points out,

It seems highly improbable that a ground created specifically for plague burial and presumably available for use by October at the latest, when weekly deaths were still running at over 4,000,[38] would not have been used extensively...References in some parish registers to burials in 'the new ground' from September 1665 could be to Bunhill Fields, though they might also be to new parochial grounds.[29]

St James' Workhouse burial ground, Broadwick Street/Carnaby Street, W1 and Golden Square W1 (Originally Pawlett's Gardens)
There are two burial grounds in the vicinity of Carnaby Street, Marshall Street and Dufour's Place. Originally there was a single burial ground for St James' parish, but this was later enlarged by the purchase of half an acre in 1693 of additional burial ground for St James' Workhouse. The two grounds together extended right through from the vicinity of Carnaby Street to the old Marshall Street baths in Dufour's Place. Both the grounds lie at the heart of tourist

43. The Soho Car Park in Poland Street. The old burial ground lies partly beneath the garage and extends back as far as Foubert's Place.

London, a few hunded yards from Carnaby Street and Regent Street.

In 1711 it is recorded that the vestry received a complaint about the smoke issuing from the chimney of Cope the gravemaker's house in the burial ground. The smoke was 'noysome and offenceive' and was caused 'by the Burning of Old Rotten Coffin Boards, and by his Wife's Frequent Laundring for People'; both activities were forbidden for the future.'[30]

Both these grounds were full by 1733. A section had been used for the building of a workhouse in 1725-7, so the ground was extended again to available land in Pesthouse Close, which no longer exists, but part of which is situated in today's Dufour's Place off Broadwick Street. An early record states of this new ground, that 'tis computed, will hold 12,000 bodies, which rot so fast that 800 may annually be buried in it. This being the only ground we could get, and the necessity of the parish requiring it, we agreed to give that rent'.[31]

The Pawlett's Garden ground, situated at 45 Foubert's Place and the Pesthouse Close ground, were incorporated into the territory of the workhouse, which lay between Poland Street and Marshall Street. The two grounds were closed in 1853 and in 1887 converted into St James's Gardens. The 1870 Ordnance Survey shows a chapel occupying part of the former burial ground.[32]

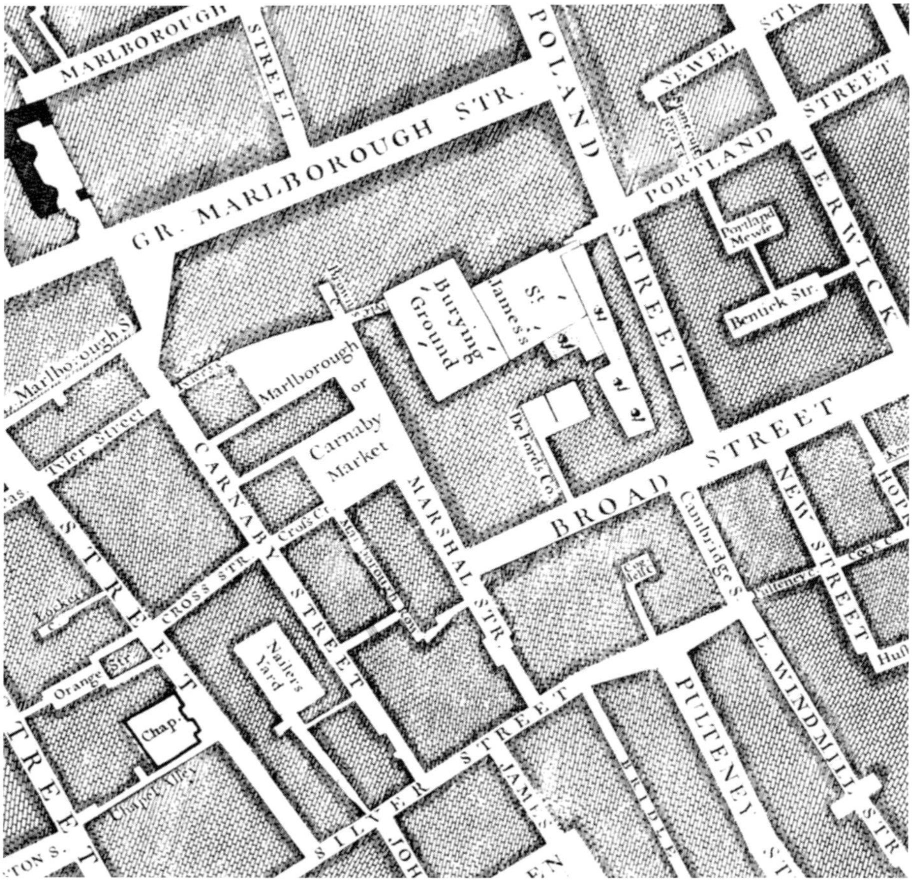

44. Rocque's map of 1746 shows the location of St James's burial ground. It was reached on the east by an entrance in Poland Street opposite Portland (now D'Arblay) Street, the site today of the Soho Car Park. 'De Fords Co.' to the south is now Dufour's Place.

Holmes noted that 'all that is left of the original ground used for interments is the garden or courtyard of the workhouse. It is a pleasant recreation ground for the inmates, and is well supplied with seats, being about ¼ acre in extent.' There were however a number of burial pits (possibly dating from the Great Plague of 1665) sunk there which 'might prove offensive and unwholesome', and these were covered over.

Infected persons were isolated in these establishments, and often, in the immediate vicinity, were buried in 'Pest Fields'. Thornbury reports that Carnaby Street was the site of a pest house, and thousands were buried nearby:

... Golden Square and Wardour Street now form the western and eastern limits. The property in this vicinity of old belonged to Lord Craven, who erected the famous pest-house here for the reception of those struck by the plague. The lazaretto itself consisted, we are told, of thirty-six small tenements; and near it, at the lower end of Marshall Street, was a common cemetery, in which some thousands of poor persons found a last resting-place during the continuance of that pestilence. Carnaby Street, which extends from the north side of the square to Great Marlborough Street, is thus described by Strype:—'An ordinary street which goes out of Silver Street, and runs northward almost to the bowling ground. On the east side of this street are the Earl of Craven's pest-houses,

45. *An area of plague burial ground at the corner of Marshall Street and Foubert's Place.*

47. *An area of burial ground. Marshall Street runs parallel on the left and Foubert's Place is straight ahead. This is the site of Pawlett's Gardens burial ground.*

46. *Dufour's Place, formerly part of Pesthouse Close. The building in the centre rear is the former Marshall Street baths, which is built on former workhouse burial ground. A builder mentioned to the author that bones had previously been unearthed on the site.*

seated in a large piece of ground, inclosed with a brick wall, and handsomely set with trees, in which are buildings for the entertainment of persons that shall have the plague, when it shall please God that any contagion shall happen'. Maitland, in his *History of London*, mentions the Pest Field in the following terms: — 'The site whereon Marshall Street, part of Little Broad Street, and Marlborough Market are now erected, was denominated the Pest Field, from a lazaretto therein, which consisted of thirty-six small houses, for the reception of poor and miserable objects of this neighbourhood that were afflicted with the direful pestilence of 1665. And at the lower end of Marshall Street, contiguous to Silver Street, was a common cemetery, wherein some thousands of corpses were buried that died of that dreadful and virulent contagion.' When Carnaby Street and other streets were built, a 'field on the Paddington estate' was assigned as a pest-field in place of that which we have described.[33]

The old Marshall Street baths (1928), now used by Westminster council, are sited at the eastern end of the burial ground.

1 Vanessa Harding, '*Epidemic Disease in London*', ed. J A I Champion (Centre for Metropolitan History Working Papers Series, No. 1, 1993): pp. 53-64.

2 Philip Ziegler, *The Black Death* (1970), pp. 159-165.

3 John Stow, *Survey of London* (1598, 1840 edn) pp. 361-362.

4 John Noorthouck, *A New History of London: Including Westminster and Southwark,* Book 1, Ch. 4 (1773), pp. 57-74.

5 Stow p. 362.

6 C J Thomas, B Sloane, *et al. Excavations at the Priory and Hospital of St Mary Spital, London.* Museum of London Archaeology Service (1997), pp.12-15.

7 Isabella (Mrs Basil) Holmes, *The London Burial Grounds* (1896), p.120.

8 http://www.molas.org.uk/pages/site SummariesDetailsAll.asp?yearsummaries2000&borough=Islington

9 Noorthouck Book 1, Ch. 14: pp. 210-230.

10 *Ibid* pp.210-230.

11 *Ibid* pp.210-230.

12 Defoe p.233.

13 *Ibid* p.235.

14 Holmes pp.124-125.

15 *Cable Trench Between Finsbury Market and Devonshire Square EC2 & EC3 TQ 33328 81459–33065 81984* MoLAS (Dan Swift) watching brief May–October 2004 EDF Energy FWD04.

16 Holmes, p.176.

17 Info ex David Orme.

18 George A. Walker, *Gatherings from Grave Yards* (1839), p.173.

19 Holmes p.127.

20 *Ibid* p.127.

21 *Ibid* pp.174-175.

22 *Tennis Court Site, The Royal London Hospital, Whitechapel Road E1 TQ 34758 81616* MoLAS (Alison Telfer) watching brief January–February 2003, Barts and the London NHS Trust RLO03.

23 Vanessa Harding on her website http://www.history.ac.uk/cmh/epiharding.html

24 *Ibid.*

25 Info. ex David Orme

26 Edward Walford, *Old & New London*, vol. IV (*c*.1875), pp. 14-26.

27 Holmes p.282.

28 Walter Thornbury, *Old & New London*, vol. II (*c*. 1873), pp. 196-208.

29 Harding, website.

30 *Survey of London, St James Westminster*, vol. XXXI (1963), pp. 209-18.

31 *Ibid.*

32 See David Orme http://doubleo.fsnet.co.uk

33 Walford, pp. 239.

CHAPTER THREE

THE WORST BURIAL GROUNDS

The overcrowding of inner London's burial grounds was not a secret. By its nature, it could not have been kept away from the eyes and noses of the public. Even so, efforts were made to hide its worst aspects. It was not unusual for private burial ground owners, eager for profit from their limited acres, to usher away mourners without the gravedigger having filled the new grave with earth, and when they had gone the body would be removed and slung in a waiting pit, usually in a disused or inconspicuous part of the ground, so that the previous grave could be used again. Many graves were several bodies deep and often the top burial was inches from the surface, or in some cases, protruded. Because of the shortage of burial space such practices could occur in parish churchyards as well as in private burial plots. As noted earlier, some of London's best known churches, such as St Margaret Westminster, St Martin-in-the-Fields and St Anne Soho, had unhygienic and offensive burial grounds. The Chadwick Report published in 1845 underlined this:

'In the metropolis, on spaces of ground which do not exceed 203 acres, closely surrounded by the abodes of the living, layer upon layer, each consisting of a population numerically equivalent to a large army of 20,000 adults, and nearly 30,000 youths and children, is every year imperfectly interred. Within the period of the existence of the present generation, upwards of a million of dead must have been interred in those same spaces.'

He continues on the consequences of so many 'imperfectly interred' corpses:

'A layer of bodies is stated to be about seven years in decaying in the metropolis: to the extent that this is so, the decay must be by the conversion of the remains into gas, and its escape, as a miasma, of many times the bulk of the body that has disappeared.'

This conclusion was undoubtedly reached by reports of the time that gravediggers sometimes perished on the spot from inhaling such gases.

In some of the populous parishes, where, from the nature of the soil, the decomposition has not been so rapid as the interments, the place of burial has risen in height; and the height of many of them must have greatly increased but for the surreptitious modes of diminishing it by removal, which, it must be confessed, has diminished the sanitary evil, though by the creation of another and most serious evil, in the mental pain and apprehensions of the survivors and feelings of abhorrence of the population, caused by the suspicion and knowledge of the disrespect and desecration of the remains of the persons interred.[1]

Reformers looked abroad to see how matters were handled in France and Germany in particular, and came to the conclusion that city burials needed to be banned. Walker's report, along with the first appearance of Dickens' *Bleak House,* resulted in the Metropolitan Interments Act of 1850, which began the process of prohibiting burials in inner London. It is worth a detailed look at some of the Walker sites, many of which still exist.

48. Appropriate theatrical publicity at the corner of Crown Court – the original entrance to the Drury Lane burial ground. The main entrance is now in Drury Lane.

The Additional ground in Drury Lane.
Now Drury Lane Gardens, Drury Lane, WC2

This additional ground to St Martin-in-the-Fields, is now situated in the heart of theatreland. As one enters from Drury Lane, on the right is the old watch house and mortuary building. Against the right hand wall, discreetly rest half a dozen extremely worn tomb stones. Buildings of a much earlier vintage than Dickens still surround the burial ground, and there is a brief history near the entrance. It was once one of the most appalling grounds in London.

George Walker in 1839 described it:

....many thousands of bodies have been here deposited. The substratum was, some years since, so saturated with dead, that the place 'was shut up' for a period. The ground was subsequently raised to its present height – level with the first floor windows surrounding the place, and in this superstratum vast numbers of bodies have, up to this period, been deposited. A short time since a pit was dug (a very common practice here) in one corner of the ground; in it many bodies were deposited at different periods, the top of the pit being covered only with boards. This ground is a most intolerable and highly dangerous nuisance to the entire neighbourhood. Rather more than two years ago, in making three areas to the centre

49. Crown Court, the original entrance to this Dickensian burial ground, situated high up behind the railings on the right.

50. The old mortuary building where bodies were kept prior to burial. The view looks towards the new, main entrance to the Gardens in Drury Lane.

51. The only visible reminders of what lies underneath in this children's playground.

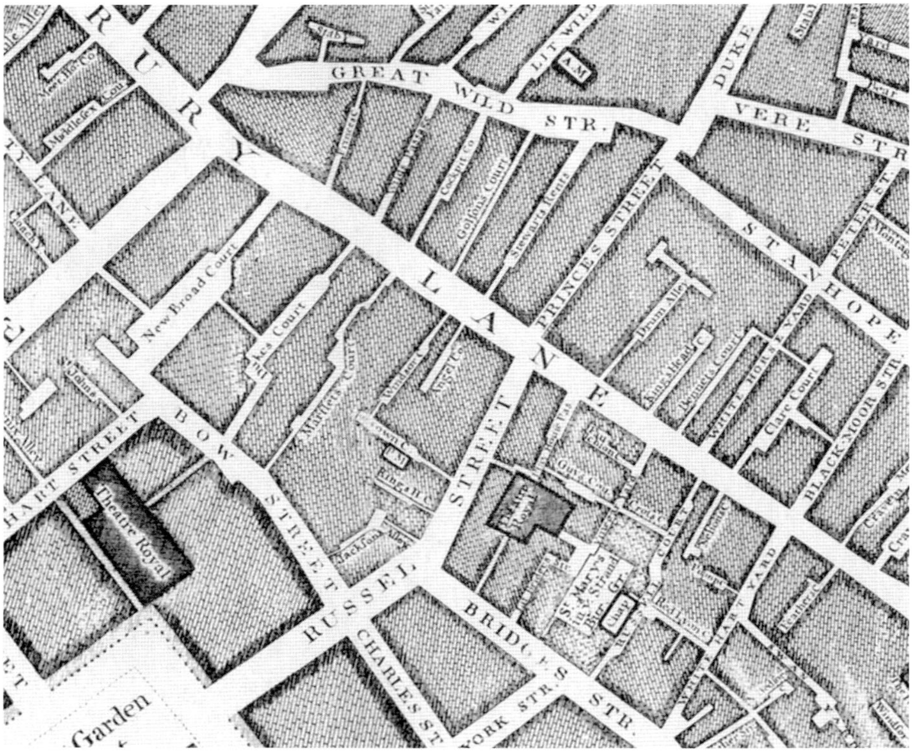

52. Rocque's map of 1746 showing the Russell Court burial ground of St Mary-le-Strand near Bridges Street

for houses on the western side of the burying ground, many bodies were disturbed and mutilated; the inhabitants of the houses are frequently annoyed by the most disgusting and repulsive sights.[2]

Holmes describes the ground in 1896 as a public garden of less than ¼ acre. 'It is well kept, and contains some gymnastic apparatus for the use of the children. Also called the Tavistock burial ground.'

Russell Court, Tavistock Street, WC2

This ground is a matter of a few hundred yards from the Drury Lane ground, but nothing of its once notorious past is evident. The section of Tavistock Street in which it was situated was in the 18th century called Russell Court. The area of the ground is still open as gardens for the red-brick flats around. George Walker had much to say about it:

Russell Court, Drury Lane. This Burying Ground belongs to the parish of St. Mary le Strand: in its original state it was below the level of the adjoining ground, – now, the surface is on a line with the first floor windows, of the houses entirely surrounding this place. It has long been in a very disgusting condition, but within the last month the surface has been 'cleaned up', and the whole may now be called 'the whited sepulchre'. A man who had committed suicide was buried here on the 20th May, 1832; the body was in the most offensive condition, and was placed within a very little distance of the surface. About twenty years ago, Mr. — —, a very respectable tradesman in the neighbourhood, was employed to make a 'cold air drain' at the west end of this ground; for this purpose it was necessary to cut through the wall of an adjoining house; on taking up the ground floor of this house, large quantities of human bones were found scattered about, – it was supposed they had been dragged thither by rats, vast numbers of which annoy the inhabitants in the proximity of this burying ground.[3]

53. The gate in the middle of the picture in Tavistock Street, approximates to the Russell Court burial ground location.

The ground was closed in 1853. By 1896, when Holmes described it, there was little to associate it with Walker's 1839 description:

430 square yards. It is probable that few grounds in London were more overcrowded with bodies than this one, which was entirely surrounded by the backs of small houses. When closed in 1853 it was in a very disgusting and unwholesome condition, and it continued to be most wretched until the Metropolitan Public Gardens Association asphalted it in 1886. It is maintained as a children's playground by the London County Council. This is the scene of 'Tom all Alone's' in *Bleak House*. There are 6 gravestones against the wall.

St Paul's, Covent Garden WC2

The church and associated burial ground lie almost at the centre of Covent Garden. Holmes records that the acre of ground given by the earl of Bedford in 1631 'is closed and very neat, the tombstones forming a flat paved yard round the church, while the rest of the ground is turfed.' Walker, in his day, saw it in a different light, when it was in a condition difficult to imagine today.

....The burying ground adjoining the church, with difficulty admits an increase. On a recent occasion, the grave digger had to make several trials before he could find room for a new tenant, and he assured me that on several occasions, he had been driven from the attempt of digging a grave, and compelled to throw back the earth, owing to the dangerous effluvia he experienced from the soil. The vault underneath the church is also crowded.[4]

54. (Top) The west front of St Paul, Covent Garden with the graveyard still intact. Watercolour at the Sir John Soane Museum, date and artist unknown.

55. Part of the burial ground has been paved over (2008).

Whitechapel Church (now the Altab Ali Park) Whitechapel Road, E1

There is now little to see unless one knows where to look. There is also nothing remaining of the church, and its site and that of its churchyard is now a public garden and renamed the Altab Ali Park. On entry there are a few tombs scattered, but otherwise the ground has been completely levelled. There is a white, chalk outline ingrained into the grass to show where the last church once stood. The churchyard was one of the most overcrowded of the early 19th century, as was its now even more hidden, and melancholic, additional ground which still remains as a plot of land behind some houses on the north side of Whitechapel Road.

The earliest record of the church dates from 1329. Originally built as a chapel-of-ease and named St Mary Matfelon, the origin of which is unknown, St Mary's Whitechapel became in 1338 the parish church for the western part of Stepney. The burial ground is probably best known for containing the remains of Richard Brandon, the supposed executioner of Charles I in 1649. Recorded in the parish register later that

56. *An 18th-century view of St Mary Matfelon, Whitechapel.*

year: "Buriall, June 21, Rich. Brandon, a man out of Rosemary Lane", now Royal Mint Street, and in the margin was added, "this R Brandon is supposed to have cut off the Head of Charles I". Brandon's burial was attended by a demonstration. A contemporary document relates,

> For the burial whereof, great store of wines were sent by the sheriff of the city of London, and a great multitude of people stood wayting to see his corpse carried to the churchyard, some crying out, 'Hang him, rogue!' 'Bury him in the dunghill!' others pressing upon him, saying they would quarter him for executing the King, insomuch that the churchwardens and masters of the parish were fain to come for the suppression of them; and with great difficulty he was at last carried to Whitechapel churchyard.[5]

57. *The outline of the old church, destroyed during the last war, is marked out in white in the present recreation ground.*

58. The site of St Mary and its churchyard is now covered by the Altab Ali Park.

On the night of 29th December 1940, the church was gutted by fire during an enemy incendiary raid, and in 1952 it was demolished altogether. In 1966 the site and the churchyard were cleared and made into a public garden.

Of Whitechapel church and its adjoining burial ground Walker had much to say, including a comment that the vaults under the church were dilapidated, and the smells coming from there, offensive. His main target, however, was the state of the burial ground, sitting alongside 'one of the greatest thoroughfares in London, and placed in the centre of a densely populated neighbourhood.'[6] He continues, suggesting that the decomposition in this overcrowded ground was the cause of much disease 'by which the lower order of the inhabitants of this parish have so frequently been visited.'

> The ground is so densely crowded as to present one entire mass of human bones and putrefaction ... It appears almost impossible to dig a grave in this ground without coming into contact with some recent interment, and the grave digger's pick is often forced through the lid of a coffin when least expected ... most of the graves are very shallow, — some entire coffins, indeed, are to be found within a foot and a half of the surface.[7]

The cavalier attitude to the dead and their remains is one of Walker's primary complaints:

> In digging a foundation for a new wall, on the eastern side of the church, the workmen penetrated through a mass of human bones eight or ten feet in thickness; these bones were thrown out, and for some time lay exposed to public view, scattered over the ground in a loathsome humid state; two or three pits were

afterwards dug to the depth of eight or ten feet, as common repositories for these bones; and the pits were filled up to within a few inches of the top, with a slight covering of earth over them; family graves also were disturbed, and many coffins exposed, – some of them literally cut in two; in consequence of which much altercation arose between the churchwardens and parishioners. Coffin wood is plentifully strewed over the ground in a rotten and decomposed state ...The poor ground, a little distance from the church, is as thickly crowded with the remains of the dead as the burying ground adjoining to the church.[8]

St Mary's Additional ground, Whitechapel Road, E1

This burial ground is anonymous but atmospheric. It is situated almost opposite the site of St Mary's church behind the row of shops and offices in Whitechapel Road. It is difficult to find. Access is via a *cul de sac* on the Whitechapel Road side of Old Montague Street. The area is slightly rundown, and surrounded by houses. The ground undulates ominously.

Walker said that this 'poor ground, a little distance from the church, is as thickly crowded with the remains of the dead as the burying ground adjoining to the church.'[9] Holmes gives us more details:

... the workhouse having been built in 1768 upon a former graveyard, and this piece to the north of it having then been set aside for interments and consecrated in 1796. The workhouse site was built upon some years ago, and the burial-ground became the playground of the Davenant Schools, one of which, the one facing St Mary's Street, was built in it; in the order for closing it, dated May 9, 1853, it is called the Whitechapel Workhouse and Schools Ground. It is difficult to say exactly how far east the burial-ground extended, but from the Ordnance map and some older plans it would appear that the recent addition to the school in Whitechapel Road has been built in the burial-ground. In 1833 the size was given as 2,776

59. Site of the St Mary's Additional ground, Whitechapel Road. In the 19th century it was described as being 'thickly crowded with the remains of the dead.'

square yards, but it was stated that in 1832 196 cholera cases were interred in an adjoining piece of ground. This is probably what is now used as a stone-yard, with carts in it.'[10]

The nearby Davenant Centre, 179-181 Whitechapel Road was, in 2005, the subject of a Museum of London watching brief when during the refurbishment of the building archaeological deposits and human remains from the post-medieval burial ground were recorded.

Burying Ground, Portugal Street, Aldwych WC2
This site was originally known as the 'Green Ground' and was one of London's most notorious burial grounds. It lay less than a minute's walk to the north of St Clement Danes church in the Strand and is now mostly under and immediately around the London School of Economics library. George Walker described it:

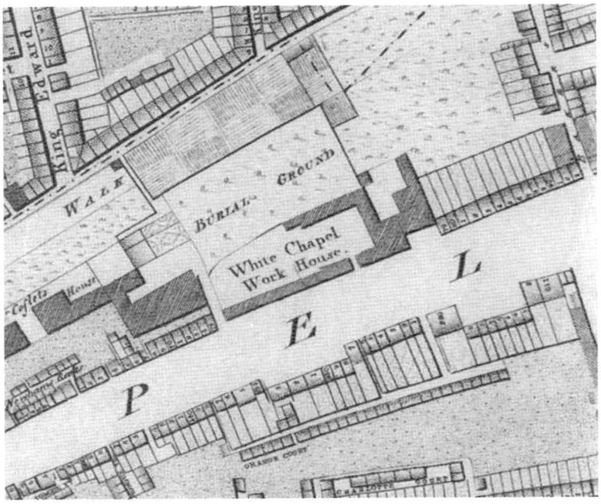

60. St Mary's Additional burial ground, behind the workhouse in Whitechapel Road, shown on Horwood's map of 1799.

61. The Almshouses' burying ground site. The Royal Courts of Justice lie immediately to the right.

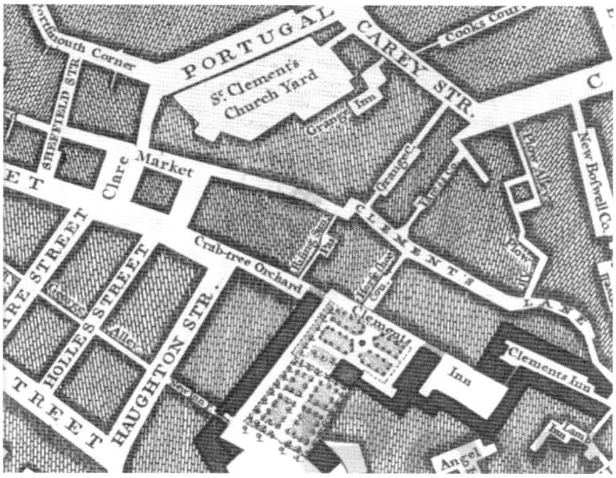

62. The burial ground at the junction of Portugal and Carey Streets, shown on Rocque's map of 1746.

This is a narrow thoroughfare on the eastern side of Clare Market; it extends from Clare Market to the Strand, and is surrounded by places, from which are continually given off emanations from animal putrescence. The back windows of the houses on the east side of the lane look into a burying ground called the 'Green Ground', in Portugal Street ... on the west side the windows (if open) permit the odour of another burying place - a private one, called Enon Chapel - to perflate the houses; at the bottom - the south end—of this Lane, is another burying place, belonging to the Alms Houses (This place is, I believe, filled with dead; many of the coffins being near the surface) within a few feet of the Strand, and in the centre of the Strand are the burying ground and vaults of St Clement Danes; in addition to which, there are several slaughter houses in the immediate neighbourhood: so that in a distance of about two hundred yards in a direct line there are four burying grounds; and the living here breathe on all sides an atmosphere impregnated with the odour of the dead. The inhabitants of this narrow thoroughfare are very unhealthy; nearly every room in every house is occupied by a separate family. Typhus fever in its aggravated form has attacked by far the majority of the residents, and death has made among them the most destructive ravages.

63. The site of the Portugal Street burial ground on the corner of Carey Street and Portugal Street. It lies under an LSE building.

This ground, which belonged to St Clement Danes, had been a 'burying place beyond the memory of man.' About 1873 it was noted:

On the south side of Portugal Street, near the centre of the few small courts that have not been swept away, stands King's College Hospital, (founded 1839) … It stands on the site of the old workhouse of St. Clement Danes, and of one of the burial-grounds already mentioned … A part of the buildings of this hospital stands on ground which, up to about the year 1850, was one of the burial-places belonging to the parish. It was about a third of an acre in extent, and called the 'Green Ground', as if in mockery. From a report of a parochial committee in 1848, we learn that upwards of 5,500 bodies had been interred within it in the previous quarter of a century. The scenes witnessed here were of the most offensive character.[11]

Walker is scathing on the state of the ground and events which took place there. He says:

The soil of this ground is saturated, absolutely saturated, with human putrescence. On Saturday the 27th April, 1839, at 5, p.m. I went, accompanied by a friend to Nos. 30 and 31, Clements Lane, and upon looking through the windows of the back attics, we saw two graves open, close to the south-eastern extremity of this burying ground. Several bones were lying on the surface of the grave nearest to us – a large piece of coffin wood was placed in readiness for removal, and, at a small distance, a heap covered with coarse sacking, was observed, which, when the covering was taken off, proved also to be long pieces of coffin wood, evidently not in a decayed state. The nails were very conspicuous ... The grave diggers were seen to take off tin plates from the coffins broken up.'[12]

The breaking up of coffins and desecration of graves were common in the name of profit. It was accepted practice to allow bodies to remain for several years until they decomposed, and then move the bones to a charnel house, thus providing extra space in the tightly packed churchyards. The 'recycling' of these graves allowed for receipt of extra burial fees, and bribes to sextons, at the expense of hygiene and dignity. Walker quotes a letter to *The Times* dated 25th June 1839:

Sir, Passing along Portugal Street on Saturday evening, about ten minutes before seven, I was much shocked at seeing two men employed in carrying baskets of human bones from the corner of the ground next the old watch-house (where there was a tarpaulin hung over the rails to prevent their being seen, and where they appeared to be heaped up in a mound), to the back of the ground through a small gate. Where this leads I do not know; but I should be glad, through the medium of your invaluable journal to ask, why is this desecration? Sir,- I feel more particularly than many might do, as I have seen twelve of my nearest and dearest relatives consigned to the grave in that ground; and I felt that, perhaps, I might at the moment be viewing, in the basket of skulls which passed before me, those of my own family thus brutally exhumed. ....'[13]

The ground was closed in 1850, and in 1855 King's College Hospital demolished the old workhouse and built a hospital which covered a large part of the site. In 1913 W H Smith & Son acquired the site, pulled down the hospital building, and replaced it with 'Strand House' which in turn became the British Library of Political and Economic Science in 1978.[14] In 1839 Walker had commented that 'the workhouse, at the north-eastern extremity of this ground, has, within the last few weeks, been disused; and the building it appears, is about to be converted into an hospital...' This is where the Royal College of Surgeons now stands.

Enon chapel: Now beneath the London School of Economics St Clement's building, St Clement's Lane, WC2

Enon Baptist chapel, opened in 1822, stood in St Clement's Lane, which connects the Strand with Portugal Street. Walker described it as being 'about midway on the western side of Clement's Lane' and surrounded on all sides by poor housing. The chapel was to cause a scandal. Charles Knight in 1851 said that '... all the marvels of the churchyard must give place to those

64. A depiction of the Enon Chapel, when later a dance hall. The condition of its burial vault, separated only by floorboards from the room above, caused a scandal from the time when it opened in 1823 until it closed in 1847. The site is now beneath the LSE. The print is from the Poor Man's Guardian, 4 December, 1847.

performed in connexion with Enon Chapel. This building is in Clement's Lane, in the Strand, and was built by the minister himself (a Dissenter) as a speculation. The upper part, opened for public worship in 1823, is separated from the lower by a boarded floor merely; and in this space (about 60 feet by 29, and 6 deep) 12,000 bodies are estimated to have been interred!'[15] The appalling overcrowding, and even worse treatment of the deceased at Enon, according to Knight, came to public attention when,

> the Commissioners of Sewers suddenly took it into their heads to compel the minister to arch it over. This was no doubt awkward; but, adapting himself admirably to circumstances, the opportunity was taken of conveying away some sixty loads of mingled earth and human remains, which were shot the other side of Waterloo Bridge, where a pathway was then forming. It may suffice to illustrate the nature of the soil removed, to observe that a few baskets-full having been thoughtlessly given away by the men employed to some labourers executing a slight street repair, a crowd were presently found round a human hand. After the stoppage of the conveniences already indicated, a new method would be required at Enon Chapel.[16]

A cabinet-maker who worshipped at the chapel between 1828 and 1835 and who testified before a Parliamentary Select Committee stated:

> At the time I attended it ... there were interments, and the place was in a very filthy state: the smell was most abominable and very injurious; I have frequently gone home myself with a severe headache, which I suppose to have been occasioned by the smell, more particularly in the summer time; also, there were insects, something similar to a bug in shape and appearance, only with wings, about the size of a small

65. The area at the top of the stairs, in Grange Court where the round building is located, is the site of the former Enon Chapel. The chapel was demolished before the First World War. Building works in 1967 produced large quantities of human bones.

bug; I have seen them in the summertime hundreds of them flying about the chapel; I have taken them home in my hat, and my wife has taken them home in her clothes; we always considered that they proceeded from the dead bodies underneath.[17]

Walker noted that:

... this [lower part] is used as a burying place, and is crowded at one end, even to the top of the ceiling, with dead. It is entered from the inside of the chapel by a trap door; the rafters supporting the floor are not even covered with the usual defence – lath and plaster. Vast numbers of bodies (... from ten to twelve thousand bodies) have been placed here in pits, dug for the purpose, the uppermost of which were covered only by a few inches of earth; a sewer runs angularly across this "burying place".[18]

Despite many complaints about the stench and the insects, the burials continued. Walker said that he had several times 'visited this Golgotha. I was struck with the total disregard of decency exhibited, — numbers of coffins were piled in confusion – large quantities of bones were mixed with the earth, and lying upon the floor of this cellar (for vault it ought not be called), lids of coffins might be trodden upon at almost every step ... I want language to express the intense feelings of pity, contempt, and abhorrence I experienced....'[19]

The chapel was still notorious enough in 1875 for Edward Walford to include a reference to its horrors in his *Old and New London* volume.

But far worse than the graveyard alluded to above, [Portugal Street burial ground] was another place of burial within the limits of this parish, long known as Enon Chapel, but afterwards converted into a chapel of ease to St Clement's, and called Clare Market Chapel. The building stands close to the eastern entrance to Clement's Inn, and the access to it is through a gateway leading into a narrow and extremely dingy court, which opens out into Carey Street. It was converted from secular to religious uses in 1823, by a Dissenting congregation, of whom Mr. Diprose writes—'These pious people, looking very naturally to ways and means, turned the vaults beneath their meeting-house into a burial-place, which soon became filled with coffins up to the very rafters, so that there was only the wooden flooring between the living youth and the festering dead, for a Sunday-school was held in the chapel as well as the congregational meeting. This state of things was allowed to continue till 1844, when a new sewer having to be carried under the building, the Commissioners of Sewers discovered the loathsome charnel-house, and had the place closed, but left the bodies to lie there and rot, heedless of all consequences. The upper premises then became tenanted by a set of teetotallers, who, amongst other uses, turned it into a dancing-room, where the thoughtless and giddy went to 'foot it' away over the mouldering remains of sad mortality, part of the bygone generation turning to dust beneath the dancers' feet.' This loathsome abomination ceased in 1847–8, when a surgeon, Mr. G. A. Walker, gained possession of the chapel with the intention of removing the remains from the vault, or 'dusthole', as it was usually called, to a more appropriate place. The work of exhumation was then commenced, and a pyramid of human bones was exposed to view, separated from piles of coffin wood in various stages of decay. This 'Golgotha' was visited by about 6,000 persons, previous to its removal, and some idea may be formed of the horrid appearance of the scene, when it is stated that the quantity of remains comprised four upheaved van loads. The whole mass of bodies was decently interred by Mr. Walker, at his own cost, in one pit in the cemetery at Norwood, the coffin wood being piled up and burnt. It is indeed strange to think that such foul abuses were not swept away until the reign of Victoria.[20]

As late as 1896 the chapel was described by Holmes as 'one of the most notoriously offensive spots in London. It was built for profit purposes and the burial fees being moderate, was extensively resorted to by the poor as a place of burial.'[21] She went on: '... no less than 20,000 coffins were deposited here. In order to accomplish this herculean task it was common practice to burn the older coffins in the minister's house, under his copper and in his fireplaces.'[22]

After being cleared by Walker the former chapel was at varying times a concert room, casino, theatre, becoming known as Clare Market Chapel around 1861.

In 1897 a Government laboratory was on the site, and in 1967 the LSE purchased it for its new St Clement's Building and uncovered 'a large quantity of human bones, among them four or five complete skulls.'[23]

St Clement Danes churchyard WC2

This historic church, almost immediately opposite the Royal Courts of Justice, is, in effect, an island in the middle of the Strand. It is within yards of the site of Enon chapel, and the 'Green Ground' in Portugal Street. Stow says of this church that ' ...In the high street, as is afore showed, is one large middle row of houses and small tenements built, partly opening to the south, partly towards the north; amongst the which standeth the parish church of St Clement Danes, so called because Harold, (1040 died) a Danish king, and other Danes were buried there ... Family intrigue led to Harold's body being 'digged out of the earth, and to be thrown into the Thames, where it was by a fisherman taken up and buried in this churchyard ...'[24] All of which, needs to be treated with some caution.

The church, and its crypt are well worth a visit. The burial ground which once surrounded the building is now concreted over, but Holmes tells us that the church 'once stood in [a] fair-sized churchyard; now ... there is only a railed-in enclosure round the church.'[25] The vault under the church has been cleared. Things were rather different when Mr Walker wrote in 1839:

ST. CLEMENT'S CHURCH, Strand. – There is a vault under this church called the 'Rector's Vault', the descent into which is in the aisle of the church near the communion table, and when opened the products of the decomposition of animal matter are so powerful,

that lighted candles, passed through the opening into the vault, are instantly extinguished; the men at different times employed, have not dared to descend into the vault until two or three days had elapsed after it had been opened, during which period the windows of the church also were opened to admit the perflation of air from the street to occupy the place of the gas emitted; – thus a diluted poison is given in exchange from the dead to the living in one of the most frequented thoroughfares of the metropolis. The other vaults underneath the church are also much crowded with dead. From some cause, at present doubtful, these vaults were discovered to be on fire ... upwards of fifty years ago; they continued burning for some days, and many bodies were destroyed.[26]

It was common to find wells in churchyards, which due to the overcrowding of burials undoubtedly led to outbreaks of disease. St Clement was no different. Walker observed that,

66. St Clement Danes c. 1800. The eastern wing of Aldwych replaced the curved row of premises on the left.

67. The vault beneath St Clement Danes in 2008.

At the eastern side of this church a pump was formerly fixed; this, within the previous month, has been removed, and a brick erection placed upon its site; the well was sunk in the year 1807, but the water had become so offensive, both to the smell and taste, that it could not be used by the inhabitants, owing, most probably, to the infiltration of the dissolved products of human putrefaction. Graves certainly have been dug very near to this well, and the land springs have risen to within a few feet of the surface.

From information recently obtained, it appears that several persons have been buried near this spot, and that in particular, the coffins of two very respectable inhabitants of the parish, as soon as let down into the graves, sunk below the surface of the water which had percolated into them; it is even stated that the deceased, from a wish to be buried in a watery grave, and knowing the situation, had particularly fixed upon it for the interment of their bodies.[27]

We have a description of the crypt dating from 1941 when Mr E A Young, a churchwarden and one-time bell-ringer there, wrote in the January 1944 edition of *The New Rambler* that:

The crypt, we found, extended under half the church and below the two vestries. It had been approached by steps on both sides. The roof is of groined vaulting, carried on brick piers and stone columns. It is very massive, yet the columns standing under the knave, in rows of three, seem to give the crypt an architectural value. The floor I could not see as it was covered with a layer of earth (probably containing human remains). An act was passed in 1851, prohibiting burials in urban areas. Shortly after this the overseers made a general clearance of the cells and their contents. The best of the coffins were re-enclosed in a newly formed chamber, and all else uniformly spread to a depth of 30 inches in a layer over the floor, always closely packed with earth, and covered with quicklime. Thus leaving all seemly, as we find it today.[28]

The crypt now is a quiet area that belies the 19th-century descriptions. The walls are lined with coffin plates.

68. St Mary-le-Strand church, 2008.

St Mary-le-Strand churchyard

Just further west in the Strand, facing the junction with Drury Lane, is St Mary-le-Strand, like St Clement's, also hemmed in by traffic. The original churchyard was more extensive than the truncated concrete area that now exists, but much was lost when the Strand was widened in the eighteenth century. The parish was the subject of claims for not handling bodies in a respectful manner, and of allowing the water from its well to be polluted by the decomposing bodies in the ground around it. Holmes commented that the churchyard was 'At the west end of the church, about 200 square yards in size, closed and not well kept.'

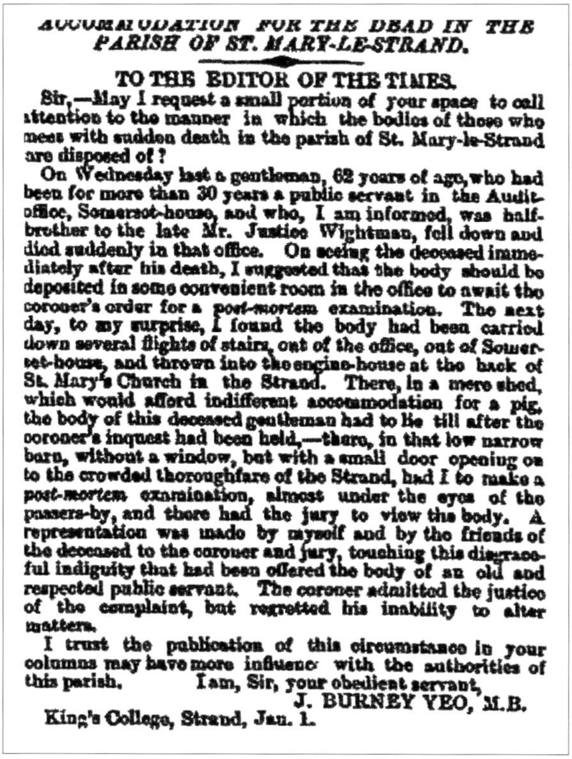

ACCOMMODATION FOR THE DEAD IN THE PARISH OF ST. MARY-LE-STRAND.

TO THE EDITOR OF THE TIMES.

Sir,—May I request a small portion of your space to call attention to the manner in which the bodies of those who meet with sudden death in the parish of St. Mary-le-Strand are disposed of?

On Wednesday last a gentleman, 62 years of age, who had been for more than 30 years a public servant in the Audit-office, Somerset-house, and who, I am informed, was half-brother to the late Mr. Justice Wightman, fell down and died suddenly in that office. On seeing the deceased immediately after his death, I suggested that the body should be deposited in some convenient room in the office to await the coroner's order for a *post-mortem* examination. The next day, to my surprise, I found the body had been carried down several flights of stairs, out of the office, out of Somerset-house, and thrown into the engine-house at the back of St. Mary's Church in the Strand. There, in a mere shed, which would afford indifferent accommodation for a pig, the body of this deceased gentleman had to lie till after the coroner's inquest had been held,—there, in that low narrow barn, without a window, but with a small door opening on to the crowded thoroughfare of the Strand, had I to make a *post-mortem* examination, almost under the eyes of the passers-by, and there had the jury to view the body. A representation was made by myself and by the friends of the deceased to the coroner and jury, touching this disgraceful indignity that had been offered the body of an old and respected public servant. The coroner admitted the justice of the complaint, but regretted his inability to alter matters.

I trust the publication of this circumstance in your columns may have more influence with the authorities of this parish.

I am, Sir, your obedient servant,

J. BURNEY YEO, M.B.

King's College, Strand, Jan. 1.

69. A letter to The Times relating to an unfortunate episode at St Mary-le-Strand in December 1868.

St Anne's Soho, Wardour Street, W1

The church was built in 1686 but mostly destroyed during the Second World War. It was not rebuilt and only the tower, which dates from 1801-1803, survives along with the churchyard. Of the latter, Walker had the following to say:

St. Ann's, Soho. – There is only one burying ground belonging to this parish; it is walled in on the side next to Princes [Wardour] Street; close to this wall is the bone house; rotten coffin wood and fragments of bones are scattered about. Some graves are only partly filled up, and left in that state, intended, probably for paupers. The ground is very full, and is considerably raised above its original level; it is overlooked by houses thickly inhabited. The inhabitants of the neighbourhood have frequently complained of the past and present condition ...

Holmes observed that a practice of playing 'skittles' with bones and skulls had frequently taken place here until exposed and stopped.[29]

The slope of the remaining burial ground to be seen in Wardour Street today indicates serious overcrowding.

70. A plaque on the north wall of St Mary-le-Strand, dated 1807, announces that a pump in the churchyard has been erected.

71. St Anne, Soho in 1828. The church was designed either by Wren or William Talman in 1677-86, and the tower erected in 1717 (rebuilt in 1803). The tower survived an air raid in 1940.

72. *St Luke's Church, Old Street, from the northern section of the churchyard, 2008.*

St Luke's Churchyard, Old Street. EC1

St Luke's has seen better days. It is on the north side of Old Street in the vicinity of a number of lost burial grounds including those of Seward Street and Bath Street. The church was badly damaged during the last war and left derelict. A clearance of the vaults took place in the 1990s, and the church was restored. The crypt is now used by the London Symphony Orchestra. St Luke's is mentioned by Walker in 1839 as a place where both crypt and churchyard overflowed:

ST. LUKE'S, Old Street:- There are three burying grounds belonging to this parish; two adjoining the church, and the poor ground, in Bath Street. Those near the church are spacious; some of the graves are very deep. The grave digger assured me, that he had often experienced the effects of the effluvia arising from the coffins, to an alarming extent, a frequent occurrence when coming suddenly upon a fresh grave, where the body had been kept too long before interment; then the effluvium would penetrate through a foot and a half or two feet of earth, and frequently produced nausea and loathing of food. He stated that many accidents arose from neglect or carelessness; a grave partly dug and left exposed for a night would, for instance, become dangerous from the collection of 'foul air'. The poor ground is at the back of the alms-houses, in Bath Street; an improved system of interment is adopted in this ground. The vaults underneath the church are less used than formerly, on account of the cemeteries round the metropolis, but the smell from these vaults is particularly offensive, - so much so, that I was informed by the Rev. Dr. Rice, the present Curate, that he never ventured to descend, but invariably performed the funeral rites whilst standing in the passage, at the top of the entrance to the vaults.[30]

Holmes observed that the churchyard was 'in two parts. Size of the whole ground, nearly 1¾ acres. The piece round the church is closed, and full of large altar tombs, ivy being planted most profusely. There is a great deal of rubbish in it.

73. *The two parts of the St Luke's churchyard, as described by Holmes in 1896. The part in the foreground contains large altar tombs, and the section through the gates to the north are laid out as a public garden.*

The part on the north side was laid out as a public garden in 1878 and is maintained by the vestry.'

St Margaret's churchyard, Westminster, SW1
The Rev. H H Milman, rector of St Margaret's, was questioned in 1843 about the state of his churchyard and whether burials should be continued there. His answer was that it was very full and that no more interments should take place there not on grounds of health but because of where it was located: 'it is a thoroughfare, and, in point of fact, it has been a cemetery so long, and is so crowded, that interment cannot take place without interfering with previous interments.'[31]

Of the now immaculately kept St Margaret's, which lies a matter of yards from both Westminster Abbey and the Houses of Parliament, Walker says, 'The ground behind the church, is too full to admit of increase, with propriety or safety.'

74. *St Margaret's, Westminster.*

75. *The churchyard of St Margaret's, Westminster today.*

Buckingham Chapel, (under Cardinal Place) Palace Street. SW1

The site of one of Walker's particularly insalubrious burial sites, situated a couple of hundred yards from Buckingham Palace, is now covered by an extensive development called Cardinal Place. Walker tells us that:

There are two vaults and a burying ground belonging to this chapel; one of the vaults is *underneath very large school rooms for boys and girls,* where some hundreds of children here receive their daily education, and the other is *underneath the chapel;* the entrance to these vaults, is through a trap-door, in the passage, dividing the school rooms from the chapel; steps lead to the bottom of the building; on the right, is the vault underneath the schools. When I visited this place a body had recently been interred, and the effluvium from it was particularly annoying. The vault is supported on wooden pillars, and there is only one grating, which fronts the street, to admit light and air; the floors of the school rooms, white-washed on the under surface, form the roof or ceiling of the vault – it is no difficult matter to see the children in the lower school room from this vault, as *there are apertures in the boards sufficiently large to admit the light from above.* This place is spacious, but very low; - the vault on the left, under the chapel, is about the same size as that under the schools, though much lower. I was assured that the ground was so full of bodies, that there was difficulty in allotting a grave; the roof of this vault, is formed by the under surface of the floor of the chapel; it is white-washed, the light passes through it; the smell emitted from this place is very offensive. In the vault underneath the chapel there are piles of bodies placed in lead; the upper ones are within a few inches of the wooden floor.

On a level with the chapel, and behind it and the school rooms, is the burial ground, which is much crowded, - most of the graves being full 7 feet deep, and nearly filled to the surface, with the dead; the ground is raised, more than six feet from the original level, – formed only by the debris of mortality. No funerals are permitted on a Sunday.

76. Cardinal Place now covers the site of a chapel and burial ground which Walker in 1839 described as being 'much crowded – most of the graves being full 7 feet deep, and nearly filled to the surface; the ground is raised more than six feet from the original level'.

Interments are allowed, in either vault, in lead or not, – if not in lead, two wooden cases are required, a shell, and an outer coffin. I could not but feel surprised that in the very atmosphere of the Palace, just a nuisance as I have just described – a nuisance pouring out the deadly emanations of human putrescence, should be allowed to exist – still more so, that it should be permitted daily to increase; it is now exposed, when will it be denounced? – surely the guardians of Her Majesty's health will not risk the consequences of neglect...[32]

Romney Street chapel, Romney Street SW1

The site of this chapel is beneath a large brick office block on the corner of Romney Street and Marsham Street, probably beneath the entrance yard. Walker commented that it was 'a Baptist place of worship, with vaults underneath, not unlike those under Buckingham chapel, but not so large. The smell from the vaults is exceedingly offensive and produces a feeling of nausea.'

77. This building in Romney Street is on the site of the former chapel, probably where the entrance courtyard is.

St James churchyard, Clerkenwell Close, EC1
The church is brooding and imposing and the area of the churchyard has built up with burials over the centuries.

Walker recorded:

CLERKENWELL CHURCH- There are four burying grounds belonging to this parish, besides a vault underneath the church; two of the grounds adjoin the church, a third is behind the prison, and the fourth, or poor ground, is in Ray Street, the entrance to which is through a private dwelling house, occupied by a broker. All these grounds are crowded, and in disorder; in the poor ground little regard is paid to the depth of the graves, or the removal of the dead. In this filthy neighborhood fever prevails, and poverty and wretchedness go hand-in-hand.[33]

As a footnote, he observed of the 'dwelling occupied by a broker' that this 'was formerly occupied by a butcher, named Rope, who had

78. (Left) St James, Clerkenwell in 1799.

79. St James today. Note the height of the burial area in the foreground in relation to the church.

his slaughter-house and stable at the back, and immediately adjoining the burial ground. About fifteen years ago, during the residence of this man, it was discovered that several bodies had been exhumed and placed in the stable, close to the slaughter-house; the inhabitants of the vicinity were powerfully excited, and the man, who had for many years carried on an extensive business, was deservedly ruined, and driven in disgrace from the neighbourhood.'

St Giles-in-the-Fields churchyard, St Giles High Street WC2

Holmes says of St Giles that 'the churchyard of St Giles' in the Fields is a very interesting one.' Writing in the last decade of the 19th century she comments that the church should really be called 'St Giles' in the Slums' and that the practices carried out in the churchyard earlier that century 'were equal to the worst anywhere – revolting ill-treatment of the dead was the daily custom.'[34]

The antiquary Thomas Pennant (1725-98) in his history of London, Westminster and Southwark (but not published until 1814) recorded that 'I have in the church yard of St. Gile's, seen with horror, a great square pit, with many rows of coffins piled one upon the other, all exposed to sight and smell; some of the piles were incomplete, expecting the mortality of the night. I turned away disgusted at the view, and scandalized at the want of police...'[36]

Walker reproduced an extract from the *Weekly Dispatch* of 30th September, 1838:

St Giles's Church Yard. – What a horrid place is Saint Giles's church yard! It is full of coffins, up to the surface. Coffins are broken up before they are decayed, and bodies are removed to the 'bone house' before they are sufficiently decayed to make their removal decent. The effect upon the atmosphere, in that very densely populated spot, must be very injurious. I had occasion to attend the church with several gentlemen, on Tuesday; being required to wait, we went into this Golgotha; near the east side we saw a finished grave, into which had projected a nearly sound coffin; half of the coffin had been chopped away to complete the shape of the new grave. A man was standing by with

80. The church of St Giles-in-the-Fields in the 18th century. Opened in 1733, it was designed by Henry Flitcroft.

a barrowful of sound wood, and several bright coffin plates. I asked him "Why is all this?" and his answer was, "O, it is all Irish". We then crossed to the opposite corner, and there is the 'bone house', which is a large round pit; into this had been shot, from a wheelbarrow, the partly-decayed inmates of the smashed coffins. Here, in this place of 'Christian burial', you may see human heads, covered with hair; and here, in this 'consecrated ground', are human bones with flesh still adhering to them. On the north side, a man was digging a grave; he was quite drunk, so indeed were

81. The 1914 Ordnance Survey shows the outline of Spa Fields burial ground as disused. The open space largely coincides with the open ground today.

all the grave diggers we saw. We looked into this grave, but the stench was abominable. We remained however, long enough to see that a child's coffin, which had stopped the man's progress, had been cut, longitudinally, right in half; and there lay the child which had been buried in it, wrapped in its shroud, resting upon the part of the coffin which remained. The shroud was but little decayed. I make no comments; every person must see the ill effects if such practices are allowed to continue.[36]

The churchyard was in the vicinity of the gallows which once stood by the main door of the church, and it contains the remains of many who were executed, in particular, those that died at Tyburn.

Spa Fields burial ground, Rosoman Place, Islington, EC1

Spa Fields today is a compact and gloomy area overlooked by flats and grey buildings of the 1970s. The ground near the chapel undulates, suggestive of its former role as one of London's most notoriously overcrowded burial grounds. In 1777 speculators leased two acres of ground from the Marquis of Northampton. It was calculated that this would provide space for 2,722 adults, but with burials taking place at 1500 per annum, after 50 years, the ground was believed to contain around 80,000 bodies. William Pinks in his *History of Clerkenwell* (1865), recorded that in 1842

82. The church in Exmouth Street that stands on the site of the former Spa Fields chapel.

...some terrible disclosures began to ooze out, proving the shameless greediness of the human ghouls who farmed the Spa Fields burial-ground. It was found that it was now the nightly custom to exhume bodies and burn the coffins, to make room for fresh arrivals. To make the new grave seven or eight bodies were actually chopped up, and corpses recently interred were frequently dragged up by ropes, so that the coffin might be removed and split up for struts to prop up the new-made graves. Bodies were sometimes destroyed after only two days' burial. A grave-digger who, being discharged, insisted on removing the body of his child, which had been recently interred, declared that he and his mates had buried as many as forty-five bodies in one day, besides still-borns. In one year they had had 2,017 funerals, and the stones of families who had purchased graves in perpetuity were frequently displaced and destroyed. The inhabitants of the neighbourhood then petitioned Parliament, complaining of the infectious smells from the burial ground, and of the shameful scandal generally ... On the night of the 14th December, 1843, an alarm was raised that the bone-house of Spa Fields ground was on fire, and the engine-keeper stated he saw in the grate a rib-bone and other bones, partly burnt, and a quantity of coffin-wood in different stages of decay. By the exertions of Mr. G. A. Walker, M.D., of the Society for the Abolition of Burials in Towns, seconded by several of the principal inhabitants, this disgraceful state of things was brought again under the attention of the magistrates, and the lessees, managers, and others were summoned to appear at the Clerkenwell Police Court, when other revolting statements were made and confirmed. At length these disgusting and loathsome practices were suppressed by law.

Walker noted that 'this ground was originally taken for a tea garden; the speculation failed, and a chapel was built upon it, in which some

83. The playground at Spa Fields on the site of the old burial ground. Photograph reproduced from Mrs Holmes' book of 1896.

ministers of the Church of England preached ...The burying ground is very large, but absolutely saturated with dead ...This place offers a difficult problem for solution; - no undertaker can explain it, except by a shrug of the shoulders.' Charles Knight, writing in 1841, observed that a parliamentary report in 1814 stated of the overflowing Spa Fields that there was 'no more space, but that you can always get a grave there'. Knight adds, '—nay graves for not less than thirty or forty persons weekly, that being frequently the number of interments.'[37]

In 1896 when Mrs Holmes was campaigning for disused burial grounds to be turned into recreation grounds, her description of the area around this burial ground was probably pertinent up to the last war: Spa Fields was now a typical London playground which was 'in the very centre of the town, although surrounded by courts and streets with such rural names as Rosoman Street, Wood Street, Pear-tree Court and Vineyard Walk - grim reminders of what the district was like a hundred years or more ago. Exmouth Street, behind which this open space is situated, is worth a visit. I was there recently, one Monday afternoon. Trucks and stalls with wares of all kinds lined the narrow road, and there seemed scarcely a square yard without a person on it. One woman was selling old garments, of which she had only about six, and these were spread out on the road itself - in the mud ... In the middle of the street is the Church of the Holy Redeemer, a huge structure in imitation of an Italian church. It stands on the site of the Spa Fields Chapel, an old round building, removed a few years ago.'

For several years, she notes, the burial ground site, once it had been closed, was used as a drill-ground by the 3rd Middlesex Rifles; and in 1885 the Metropolitan Public Gardens Association entered into negotiations with the owner, the Marquis of Northampton, and he generously handed it over at a nominal rental for the purposes of a children's playground and subsequently added to it half an acre of adjoining land.'[40]

84. The west side of St Botolph's and the area of the 1665 plague pit mentioned by Defoe.

St Botolph's Aldgate. Aldgate High Street, EC3
St Botolph's stands at the junction of Houndsditch and Aldgate High Street. It is probably of Saxon origin. A plague pit mentioned by Defoe lies to the west of the church. The Metropolitan Public Gardens Association laid out Aldgate churchyard in 1892.

The following report from the *Weekly Dispatch* of the 9th September 1838 refers to the burial area at the north side of the church:

TWO MEN SUFFOCATED IN A GRAVE

On Friday evening, an inquest was held in the Committee Room of the Workhouse, of the parish of St. Botolph's, Aldgate, on the bodies of Thomas Oakes, the grave digger belonging to Aldgate church, and Edward Luddett.— Mr. Edward Cheeper, the master of the workhouse, stated, that about eleven o'clock,

85. The north side of St Botolph's, where two grave diggers died in 1838.

while passing through Church Passage, Aldgate, he heard the loud screams of a female in the church yard, and he hastened to the spot, and looking into the grave, about twenty feet deep, at the North side of the church yard he saw the deceased grave digger, Oakes, lying on his back apparently dead. A ladder was instantly procured, and the deceased young man, Luddett, who by this time, with several others, had been attracted to the spot, instantly volunteered to descend to the assistance of Oakes. On his reaching the bottom of the grave, witness called out to him to place the ropes under the arms of Oakes, and the instant he stooped to raise the head of Oakes, he appeared as if struck with a cannon ball, and fell back with his head in a different direction to his fellow sufferer, and appeared instantly to expire. King, the former grave digger, made two or three ineffectual attempts to descend, but so foul was the air, that he was obliged to be drawn up again, and it was a full twenty-five minutes, or half an hour, before the bodies were taken up by means of a hook attached to a rope...[39]

The inquest then established that this 'deep grave' being a 'pauper's grave' had been open for about four weeks. A witness, associated with the church stated that

....such graves as those were kept open until there were seventeen or eighteen bodies interred in them; there was only the body of a still-born infant in the one in question. It was not the custom to put any earth between the coffins in those graves, except in cases where the persons died of contagious diseases, and in that case some slaked lime and a thin layer of earth were put down to separate them...

Mr Townley, a tradesman residing close to the church, complained of the practice adopted in the churchyard, 'which he said was most distressing to the sight, and injurious to the health of the inhabitants of that crowded neighbourhood, and he hoped something would be done about it.'

Globe Fields, Whitechapel (now Globe Road Memorial Gardens) E2

The Globe Fields burial ground remains today, in truncated form, a mute testimony to one of the worst burial ground scandals of the 19th century. In evidence before a Parliamentary Select Committee of 1842, the ground was described as being half an acre in extent. Holmes wrote that 'over half of the Globe Fields ground the Great Eastern Railway runs; the remainder is a bare yard, with several miserable tomb-stones in it and quantities of rubbish. It is fast closed behind an iron gate of colossal proportions, and it daily becomes more neglected and untidy.'[40] In 2008 what remains of the ground is still untidy and neglected. The gates are locked but the ground is easily visible from Globe Road.

A *Morning Post* article of Monday, 14 October 1839 said of this burial ground:

86. The Globe Road Memorial Gardens, scene of some of the worst excesses of 19th-century burial ground practices.

INDECENT DISINTERMENT OF DEAD BODIES. – Since Friday, a good deal of excitement has prevailed in the neighbourhood of Globe Lane, Mile-end, in consequence of the interference of the police to prevent the indecent disinterment of bodies in the burial ground behind Globe Fields Chapel. It appeared that Mr. Poole, a clerk in the service of the Eastern Counties Railway Company, being stationed on that part of the railroad which runs close to the burial ground in question, had observed two men and a boy exhuming the bodies buried in one part of the ground, and hurling them, in the most indecent manner, and indiscriminately, into a deep hole, which they had previously made at another part; and considering such a proceeding as somewhat extraordinary, as well as exceedingly indecent, he felt it to be his duty to call at the police station-house, in the Mile-end Road, and give information of what he had witnessed. Inspector M'Craw, accompanied by sergeants Parker and Shaw ... proceeded to the burial ground in question, and as they were about to enter, they met a lad with a bag of bones and a quantity of nails, which he said he was going to sell. On examining them, the nails were evidently those which had been taken out of coffins, and the bones seemed to be those of human beings, but the lad denied that they were so, though he acknowledged the nails to have been taken from the coffins. The inspector and sergeants then proceeded to an obscure corner of the ground, and found there a great number of bodies, packed one upon another, in a very deep grave which had been dug to receive them, and the uppermost coffin was not more than seven or eight inches, at the utmost, from the surface ... On making inquiries, it appeared that the ground was the property of an undertaker, residing in the neighbourhood of Bishopsgate Street; that owing to the low rate of fees, and affording a protection against resurrection men, by being surrounded by high walls, a great number of burials took place; but as few would select the remote corner as a place of rest for their friends or relations, it was used for the purpose of removing the bodies of those buried in the better and more crowded part of the ground to make room for others. The officers said that the dreadful stench emitted from the half-decomposed bodies, placed in the hole before mentioned, was sufficient to engender disease in the neighbourhood, upon which the men immediately set about covering them.'[41]

A gravedigger at the ground was interviewed by the Select Committee.

Chairman: What is your occupation? – A jobbing, labouring man, when I can get anything to do.

Chairman: *Have you been a gravedigger in Globe, Mile End?*

Yes

Chairman: *Is that a private burying-ground?*

Yes.

Chairman: *To whom does it belong?*

Mrs. Thomas Tagg.

Chairman: *Have many pits been dug in it for the depositing of bodies previously interred?*

Yes.

Chairman: *Where did they come from?*

Out of the coffins which were emptied for others to go into the graves.

Chairman: *Were they bones, or bodies, that were interred?*

Yes; the bones and bodies as well

Chairman: *Were they entire, or in a state of decomposition?*

Some were dry bones, and some were perfect.

Chairman: *What did you do with them?*

Chucked them into a pit.

Chairman: *How many bodies did you chuck in?*

I cannot say, they were so numerous; each pit would hold about a dozen.

Chairman: *How many of these pits did you dig?*

I suppose I dug a matter of 20 myself.

Chairman: *How near to the surface of the earth did these dead bodies or bones come?*

Within about two feet.

Chairman: *What is the size of this ground?*

It is rather better than half an acre.

Chairman: *How many bodies are buried in that ground within a year?*

I cannot say; I suppose there are 14,000 have been buried in that ground.

Chairman: *How long has it been open?*

Since the year 1820.[42]

St Dunstan's churchyard, Whitehorse Lane, Stepney E1

The church of St Dunstan was founded in 960. The burial ground is large and contains an area at the southern end, now used for dog walking, that is the site of one of Defoe's 1665 plague pits.

87. The churchyard of St Dunstan, Stepney, showing how high the vast numbers of burials had raised the land surrounding the church.

88. The site of the plague pit in the churchyard of St Dunstan. This area is marked by a sign designating it as the 'dog exercise area'.

Walker in 1839 described the ground as 'crowded to excess; footpaths cross through it in every direction. The soil, largely imbued with the products of putrefaction, is also extremely moist; many of the tomb-stones have sunk deeply in the earth. Here the peculiar putrefactive odour may be frequently distinguished ...'

Holmes stated that the ground was of about 6 acres and that at the time of plague around 150 bodies were interred there daily. Hillocks and undulations have left the church itself lying well below the level of the churchyard.

The St Dunstan churchwardens met in February 1625/6, a plague period in London,to decide where sand and gravel could be dug so 'that the churchyard may be speedilie earthed over'. The Stepney churchyard was by then more than overfull. The vestry in the same month recorded the situation plainly: 'the old Churchyard will affoord no more convenient place of Buriall without danger of Infection by reason of the noisomenes of the ground there so opened by reason of so many bodies formerlie enterred there.'

In April the vestry, still concerned by the number of burials taking place near the church, decided to restrict them. Having directed where burials could be made, it noted that the sexton was to be fined if he dug graves anywhere else.[43]

1 Edwin Chadwick, *A report on the results of a special inquiry into the practice of interment in towns, etc,* (1845) ed. by C. Sherman, p.27.
2 George A. Walker, *Gatherings from Grave Yards* (1839), pp.162-3
3 Walker pp.163-4
4 Walker p.164
5 John Timbs, *Curiosities of London: exhibiting the most rare and remarkable objects of interest in the Metropolis* (1855). p.146
6 Walker p.168
7 Walker pp.168-9
8 Walker pp.168-9
9 Walker p.169
10 Isabella (Mrs Basil) Holmes, *The London Burial Grounds* (1896), p.13.
11 Edward Walford, *Old and New London*, vol. III (*c.* 1875), pp. 26-32.
12 Walker p.150
13 Walker p.151
14 G. Howarth and P. Jupp, 'Enon Chapel' in *The changing face of death: historical accounts of death and disposal* (1997), p.95.
15 Charles Knight, *London* vol. iv (1841, 1851 edn) p.164
16 Knight, p.164
17 Howarth and Jupp, p. 95
18 Walker p.155
19 Walker p.157
20 Walford, pp. 31-32.
21 Holmes p.193
22 Holmes p.193-4
23 Howarth and Jupp p.103
24 John Stow, *Survey of London* (1598, 1840 edn.), p.64
25 Holmes p.104
26 Walker p.158
27 Walker pp.158-160
28 William Kent, The Lost treasures of London (1947), p.20
29 Holmes p.98
30 Walker pp.174-5
31 Chadwick, p.142
32 Walker p.184-5
33 Walker p 175-6
34 Holmes p.108
35 Thomas Pennant, *Some account of London, Westminster and Southwark* (1813), p.157
36 Walker p.164-5
37 Knight, p.168
38 Holmes 274-5
39 *Weekly Dispatch*, 9 September 1838 quoted from Walker pp. 138-140
40 Holmes, pp.197-198
41 Walker, pp.199-200
42 Quoted from Holmes (modified) pp. 194-196
43 Hill and Frere, *Memorials of Stepney Parish* (1890).

CHAPTER FOUR

SOME HISTORIC BURIAL GROUNDS

The Tower of London, EC3

Mrs Holmes observed that there were four recognised burial places associated with the Tower of London. These were the churchyard of St Peter ad Vincula, the vaults that lie beneath that church, a strip by its eastern wall, and other areas within the Tower precinct where '... it is probable that burials took place in a somewhat promiscuous fashion.'[1] The best known 'promiscuous burial' was that of the murdered princes who were buried at the foot of the White Tower, 'meetly deep in the ground, under a great heap of stones'. The remains were discovered in 1674 and moved to Westminster Abbey. Within the church itself lie some of the execution victims of Tower Hill and Tower Green.

There was another small burial ground related to the Tower. It is shown on the 1872 Ordnance Survey map, just outside the wall. It was demolished for the construction of Tower Bridge.

89. The 1872 Ordnance Survey map shows a 'Burial Ground (Disused)', to the right and just below the word 'Ditch'. The approach to Tower Bridge is now on most of its ground.

90. The area of the Tower burial ground just outside the wall of the Tower. Tower Bridge is on the right, looking south to north at the eastern end of the Tower.

St Olave's, Hart Street, EC3

Situated not far from Tower Hill, St Olave's churchyard is probably one of the most atmospheric remaining in the City of London, and has an interesting history. Stow at the end of the 16th century described it as a 'proper parish church ...'[2]

Holmes noted that 'The church itself is one of the most beautiful pieces of ecclesiastical architecture in London – a small Gothic building, admirable in its proportion. The old gate of the churchyard has skulls and cross-bones on it, and in this ground were interred a vast number of the victims of the plague of 1665 ...'[3] A visitor in 2008 notices on entering the tiny building from the churchyard that the entry to the church is downwards, indicating the depth of burials outside over the centuries.

Charles Dickens wrote in his *The Uncommercial Traveller*:

One of my best beloved churchyards, I call the churchyard of Saint Ghastly Grim; touching what men in general call it, I have no information. It lies at the heart of the City, and the Blackwall Railway shrieks at it daily. It is a small small churchyard, with a ferocious, strong, spiked iron gate, like a jail. This gate is ornamented with skulls and cross-bones, larger than the life, wrought in stone; but it likewise came into the mind of Saint Ghastly Grim, that to stick iron spikes a-top of the stone skulls, as though they were impaled, would be a pleasant device. Therefore the skulls grin aloft horribly, thrust through and through with iron spears. Hence, there is attraction of repulsion for me in Saint Ghastly Grim, and, having often contemplated it in the daylight and the dark ...[4]

In this same church was buried Thomas Pepys, brother of the diary-keeper, whose funeral Samuel records with a curious mixture of grief, thrift, and want of feeling. Samuel's diary entry notes some curious customs of the period:

91. Wrote Dickens of St Olave's churchyard, 'This gate is ornamented with skulls and cross-bones, larger than the life, wrought in stone ...'

18th March, 1664. Up betimes, and walked to my brother's, where a great while putting things in order against anon; and so to Wotton, my shoemaker, and there got a pair of shoes blacked on the soles against anon for me; so to my brother's. To church, and, with the grave-maker, chose a place for my brother to lie in, just under my mother's pew. But to see how a man's tombes are at the mercy of such a fellow, that for sixpence he would, as his own words were, 'I will justle them together but I will make room for him,' speaking of the fulness of the middle aisle, where he was to lie; and that he would, for my father's sake, do my brother, that is dead, all the civility he can; which was to disturb other corps that are not quite rotten, to make room for him; and methought his manner of speaking it was very remarkable, as of a thing that now was in his power to do a man a courtesy or not. I dressed myself, and so did my servant Besse; and so to my brother's again; whither, though invited, as the custom is, at one or two o'clock, they come not till four

92. St Olave's churchyard where Pepys saw the dead piled high during the Great Plague. Note the height of the ground above the church door.

or five. But, at last, one after another they come, many more than I bid; and my reckoning that I bid was 120, but I believe there was nearer 150. Their service was six biscuits apiece, and what they pleased of burnt claret. My cousin, Joyce Norton, kept the wine and cakes above, and did give out to them that served, who had white gloves given them ... Anon to church, walking out into the street to the conduit, and so across the street; and had a very good company along with the corps. And being come to the grave as above, Dr. Pierson, the minister of the parish, did read the service for buriall; and so I saw my poor brother laid into the grave; and so all broke up; and I and my wife, and Madam Turner and her family, to her brother's, and by-and-by fell to a barrell of oysters, cake, and cheese, of Mr. Honiwood's, with him, in his chamber and below, being too merry for so late a sad work. But, Lord! to see how the world makes nothing of the memory of a man an hour after he is dead! And, indeed, I must blame myself, for though at the sight of him dead, and dying, I had real grief for a while, while he was in my sight, yet, presently after, and ever since, I have had very little grief indeed for him.[5]

93. St Bartholomew the Less, inside the gates of the hospital. The concreted area was once a burial ground.

When Pepys revisited the church on 30 January 1665/6, he recorded that 'it frighted me indeed ... more than I thought it could have done, to see so many graves lie so high upon the churchyard where people have been buried of the plague. I was much troubled at it, and do not think to go through it again a good while.'[6]

Smithfield, EC1

The area around Smithfield and St Bartholomew's hospital is dense with early burial grounds. In the immediate vicinity of the hospital alone there are four. One is situated, beneath the roadway tarmac, within the hospital entrance adjacent to St Bartholomew the Less church. According to Holmes, it once extended further south. The 1746 Rocque map indicates that open ground to the north-east was probably burial ground. Another ground belonging to St Bartholomew the Less is beneath the west wing of the hospital which was built in the middle of the eighteenth century. Another ground for the same church is possibly situated under the hospital's central courtyard and a fourth cemetery is shown on Rocque's map, but by the end of the eighteenth century was built on.[7]

The church of St Bartholomew the Great is west of the hospital and is reached via a pathway which runs through a churchyard several feet high from centuries of burials. The church is the remnant of a priory, founded in 1123 and suppressed at the Dissolution of the Monasteries, at which time the nave was taken down. The area around the church comprises a series of burial grounds, now mostly built over.

To the north was the burial ground for the monastery. The enclosed garden area to the south flanked the old cloisters. Holmes says that 'the Priory had a cemetery attached which is covered by the buildings near the south transept of the church. Commenting on an excavation, the Museum of London noted that

Remains of the Chapter House and slype [covered passage way] of the Priory were found in the south-

94. *St Bartholomew the Great and Cloth Fair, with one of the local burial grounds in 1828.*

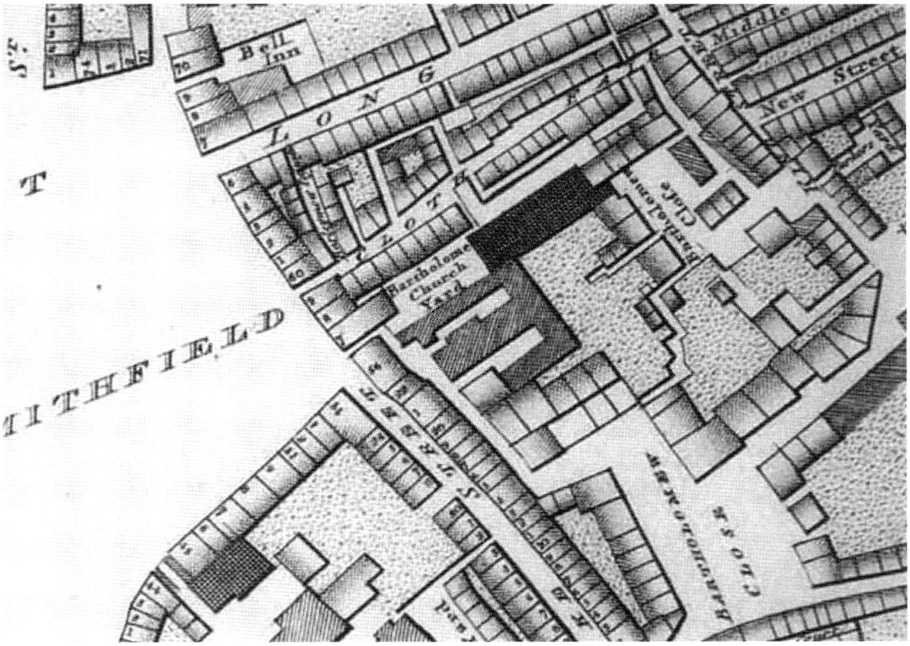

95. Horwood's map of 1799 showing Bartholomew Close and St Bartholomew churchyard.

96. Excavations in 1998 at 43 Bartholomew Close, centre, the former site of the Chapter House, revealed the partial remains 'of at least three inhumations'.

western half of the site, post-dating an earlier medieval rubbish pit ... Within the Chapter House the partial remains of at least three human inhumations were recorded, parts of which are still *in-situ* beneath the present slab. More burials are expected to survive on the site. To the north of the Chapter House is an early cemetery, of which the remains of three probably 12th-century burials were recorded. In the north-western part of the site the cemetery appears to have been partly cleared during the later 12th century. The remains of a right-angle foundation was recorded in the area of the early cemetery.[8]

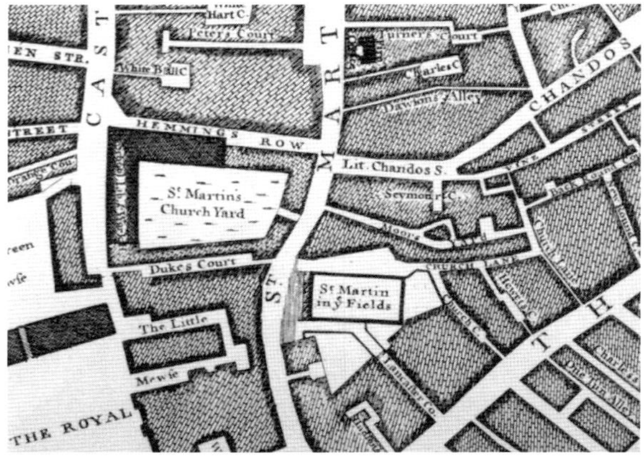

98. Rocque's map of 1746 showing the burial ground opposite St Martin-in-the-Fields church.

St Martin-in-the-Fields, Trafalgar Square, WC2

Harvey Hackman in his book on London churchyards says of this burial ground that it is peculiar in that St Martin 'has retained no grass or garden round its walls ... situated where it is, it is not surprising that it has lost most of its churchyard.' Nell Gwynne who died in 1687, and Jack Sheppard executed in 1742 at Tyburn, were both buried in the now asphalted area that was once a churchyard. A good number of interments were removed to St Martin's extra-mural burial ground in Camden Town, a graveyard which is itself now a public garden (see chapter five). Of the old churchyard, Walker

97. St Martin-in-the-Fields, 2008, with the National Gallery in the foreground. Part of the eastern section of the gallery is on the old burial ground of St Martin's.

observed that it had been 'broken up for the purpose of making improvements in the city of Westminster; the dead were disinterred, and their remains removed to vaults, called catacombs.' This circumstance is commemorated by the following inscription, on the north side of the church:

These catacombs were constructed at the expense of the Commissioners of His Majesty's Woods and Forests, in exchange for part of the burial ground of this parish, on the south side of the church ...

An article in the *Sunday Times* of 12 June, 1831, quoted by Walker, gives us an idea of how the repose of the dead could be turned into a tourist attraction.

The new vaults under St Martin's burying ground are the most capacious structure of the sort in London. They were opened on Tuesday, at the consecration of the new burial ground. They consist of a series of vaults, running out of one another in various directions; they are lofty, and when lighted up, as on Tuesday, really presented something of a comfortable appearance. Some of the vaults having been quite filled with the coffins taken out of the old burying grounds, have been blocked up at both ends ... There are arcades or corridors leading to the vaults, which branch off right and left, along which are ranges of head-stones, recording the names of individuals whose bones, removed from their old resting place, repose beneath ... Crowds of ladies perambulated the vaults for some time, and the whole had more the appearance of a fashionable promenade than a grim repository of decomposing mortality.'[9]

Allhallows' Staining, Mark Lane, EC3

Of this church, only the tower remained when Mrs Holmes carried out her survey. The church, in Mark Lane dated from at least the 12th century. Having survived the Great Fire of 1666 the church

99. The church of All Hallows Staining in Mark Lane in 1870, shortly before its demolition, save for the 15th-century tower, which still survives.

collapsed in 1671 probably because the number of burials too close to its walls undermined it. The tower had survived and the rest of the church was rebuilt in 1674-5. In 1870 All Hallows, but not the tower, was demolished – even in those more pious days its congregation numbered only 25 – and the churchyard cleared of interments and levelled to form a garden for the Clothworkers' Company.

Holmes described a 'neatly kept little burial ground' which lay in the centre.

St Paul's Cathedral churchyard EC4

Until the 17th century, the churchyard area of St Paul's was probably London's best known meeting, preaching and commercial venue, as well as being used for the execution of some of the perpetrators of the 1605 Gunpowder Plot. It was entirely enclosed by a wall in 1285, which ran from 'Ave Maria Lane eastward along Paternoster Row to the old Exchange, Cheapside, and then southwards to Carter Lane, at the end of which it turned to Ludgate Archway.'[10] In the reign of Edward II, (1307- 27) the churchyard was a refuge of thieves and prostitutes. As Holmes observed, 'the Churchyard was not only a religious centre, but was also a very worldly one. Many unseemly scenes used to take place there, and the ground was walled in because it was becoming the resort of those who did not behave themselves properly...'[11]

In 1549 Edward Seymour, Protector Somerset, demolished the cloister, chapel, and charnel house to provide him with the materials needed for his new mansion, Somerset House, in the Strand. From the charnel house, Stow tells us that one thousand cartloads of bones were taken away and buried in Finsbury Field, later to become Bunhill. Thornbury in *Old and New London* describes the appearance of the churchyard:

The cloister was full of monuments, and above was a library. In an enclosure east of this stood the College of Minor Canons; and at Canon Alley, east, was a burial chapel called the Charnel, from whence

100. The north side of St Paul's churchyard, with the end of Cheapside. In the foreground on the left is a trunk manufacturer's premises and a group of figures looking through the window of Bowles and Carver's print shop.

101. An early view of Paul's Cross, published in 1809. The Cross was taken down in 1643.

Somerset sent cart-loads of bones to Finsbury Fields. East of Canon Alley stood Paul's Cross, where open-air sermons were preached to the citizens, and often to the reigning monarch. East of it rose St Paul's School and a belfry tower, in which hung the famous Jesus bells, won at dice by Sir Giles Partridge from that Ahab of England, Henry VIII. On the south side stood the Dean and Chapter's garden, dormitory, refectory, kitchen, slaughterhouse, and brewery. These eventually yielded to a cloister, near which, abutting on the cathedral wall, stood the chapterhouse and the Church of St Gregory. Westward were the houses of the residentiaries; and the deanery, according to Milman, an excellent authority, stood on its present site. The precinct had six gates – the first and chief in Ludgate Street; the second in Paul's Alley, leading to Paternoster Row; the third in Canon Alley, leading to the north door; the fourth, a little gate leading to Cheapside; the fifth, the Augustine gate, leading to Watling Street; the sixth, on the south side, by Paul's Chain. On the south tower of the west front was the Lollards' Tower, a bishop's prison for ecclesiastical offenders ...[12]

As Thornbury records, within the old churchyard was Paul's Cross, situated at the north-east corner. This was an outdoor pulpit used for public announcements and preaching. It remained until 1643 when Parliament ordered its destruction. A monument now stands near the original site.

Christ Church, Spitalfields E1

The church, designed by Nicholas Hawksmoor, is situated almost directly opposite the old Spitalfields Market in Commercial Street. Walker said of this churchyard that it 'is literally overcharged with dead. The vault underneath the body of the church is also very much crowded.'

In the late eighteenth century the churchyard consisted of three parts, 'the best Ground' at the west end, 'the Middle Ground', and 'the lower

102. St Paul's churchyard with the replacement for Paul's Cross, in 2008.

103. The old burial ground now lies under the Christ Church Gardens Youth and Community Centre. Gravestones line the playground's perimeter.

104. *Christ Church, Spitalfields, 2008.*

and Poor Ground' at the east end. By 1791 it had become necessary to enlarge the area 'heretofore set apart and appropriated for the Interment of the Poor' by the addition of a strip of ground under the south wall, and 'that a Row of Trees be planted by way of boundary to ascertain the same'.

The *Survey of London*, in its history of the area, noted that:

In 1859 the Commissioners of Works agreed to grant a lease to the Whitechapel District Board of Works of a piece of ground on the east side of Commercial Street, to be added to the churchyard, which was thereby extended to front the new street. In June of the same year the churchyard was closed for burials, which had been prohibited in the vaults under the church from April of the previous year. By a faculty from the Bishop of London of 18 June 1859 the churchyard was authorized to be used as a 'Lawn or Ornamental Ground ... to secure an open space in the midst of a crowded and dense population'. It was to be enclosed from the road by 'a lofty and substantial iron railing ... Most of the monuments in the churchyard were removed and some of the trees felled by the Stepney Borough Council in 1950.[13]

In 2003 the Museum of London carried out an excavation at Christ Church, examining the contents of the vaults. Three small vaults at the east end of the crypt were opened, and 78 burials recorded. The assorted coffins and bones, generally in a poor condition, were removed.[14]

1 Isabella (Mrs Basil) Holmes, *The London Burial Grounds* (1896), p.69.
2 John Stow, *Survey of London* (1598, 1840 edn.), p.127.
3 Holmes p.78.
4 Charles Dickens, *The Uncommercial Traveller* chap. 23.
5 Pepys quoted in Walter Thornbury, *Old and New London*, vol. II, (c. 1873), pp.107-116.
6 *Ibid* pp. 107-116.
7 I am grateful to David Orme for his concise summary of a complex series of burial grounds in the vicinity of the hospital and church.
8 http://www.molas.org.uk/pages/siteSummariesDetailsAll.asp?year=summaries1998.
9 George A. Walker *Gatherings from Grave Yards* (1839) pp.161-162.
10 Walter Thornbury, *Old and New London*, vol. I (1873), pp. 262-274.
11 Holmes p.59.
12 Thornbury, pp.262-274.
13 *Survey of London*: vol. 27: *Spitalfields and Mile End New Town* (1957), pp.148-169.
14 'Three Vaults, Christ Church, Spitalfields E1' TQ 3377 8178 MoLAS (Adrian Miles) excavation January – February and May 2003 The Rector and the Parochial Church Council of Christ Church Spitalfields and the Christ Church Spitalfields Restoration Trust CSM03.

CHAPTER FIVE

CLOSED AND LOST BURIAL GROUNDS

Mrs Holmes in 1896 estimated that at least forty churchyards had, in the City of London alone, disappeared, the result, she concluded of the dissolution of the priories, the formation of new streets, and the invasion of railways. Among the more notable disappearances was the Jews' original burial-ground in and around Jewin Street. Farringdon Market, and Farringdon Avenue were built over the workhouse ground, Shoe Lane, which belonged to St Andrew's, Holborn. The graveyard of St John, Cloak Lane, was taken by the District Railway in 1879 for Cannon Street station, as was that of St Mary Bothaw. Another ground that disappeared beneath St Bartholomew's Hospital was the additional ground to Christ Church, Moorgate Street – it lay under the southern end of the hospital. Mansion House station is on the site of the burial ground for Holy Trinity the Less, Trinity Lane. Liverpool Street station was formerly the site of the Bethlem burial ground. London Bridge and Charing Cross railway stations are both situated on top of Friends' burial grounds. The Flemish burial ground in Carter Lane, EC4 disappeared beneath the approach to London Bridge station.

The Mercers' Hall in Ironmonger Lane sits on top of the ground of St Thomas Acon, and the Mansion House straddles the site of St Mary Woolchurch Haw and its ground. Part of the National Gallery in Trafalgar Square is on the additional ground of the nearby St Martin-in-the-Fields. Off the Strand, the present Somerset House is on top of the old Somerset House cemetery and that of the original church of St Mary-le-Strand. Alongside Tower Bridge is the sprawling area of St Katharine's Docks, which covers the former burial ground of St Katharine's Hospital and its additional ground. The old Royal Mint at Tower Hill occupies the site of a Pest Field, or burial ground used for those that died in the nearby Pest House. Similarly, Petticoat Lane in Whitechapel straddles a Pest Field. Spital Square is host to an extensive area of burials as it, and much of the surrounding area, was built on the burial ground for St Mary Spital priory.

St John the Evangelist churchyard, Smith Square, SW1

Smith Square, close to Westminster Abbey, is dominated by the imposing St John's church at its centre. The church, designed by Thomas Archer, and built 1713-28, was badly damaged in the last war and is now a public hall mostly used for concerts. The crypt has been cleared and is now a café, and the area around the church once used for burials now lies beneath the road. Holmes, in 1896 tells us that 'This churchyard used to extend, at the beginning of the century, for some distance on the south side of the church, but was thrown into the road. Now all that remains is a very small bare enclosure, not ¼ acre in size, railed in round the church.'

Additional ground for St John the Evangelist, St John's Gardens, Horseferry Road, SW1

These gardens are extensive and well maintained. On entry there is a brief history of the gardens as a burial ground. The plaque states that during a 10-year period alone, presumably in the 18th century, '5126 graves had been dug …' A wall was built round the

105. *The church of St John in Smith Square. Much of its burial ground is now beneath the road.*

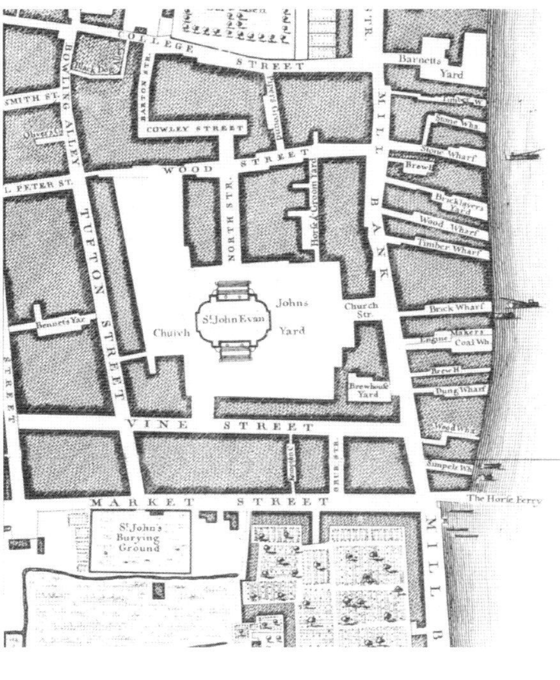

106. *Rocque's map of 1746 showing the St John's Additional burial ground in what is now Horseferry Road.*

ground in 1784, probably to hinder the 'resurrectionists' for whom the ground was a frequent source of attention. There are some tombstones laid out against the north. Despite its size, it soon became overcrowded and additional earth was on three occasions added to build up the ground and allow additional burials. It was extended in 1823 and closed in 1853 by Lord Palmerston on the grounds that it had become 'a great public nuisance.' The ground was curtailed and landscaped after road widening in 1884. Walker commented that this ground was 'very spacious and overcrowded; the churchwardens have been obliged to give up a part of the ground, for the interment of the poor, which had formerly been set apart for the more fortunate. The soil here is very damp, and, at a shallow depth, the water flows in abundantly;

107. St John's Additional burial ground, now St John's Gardens, off Horseferry Road, 2008. 'It was much used for the burial of soldiers, and was much overcrowded.'

the depth of the graves varies from four to eight feet.'[1] Holmes said that it was 'very much used, especially for the burial of soldiers. It is 1½ acres in size, and has been laid out as a public garden. It is neatly kept by the vestry, and much frequented.'

Poor-ground, Bath Street, EC1

This former burial ground of the Pesthouse that stood almost opposite in Bath Street is still open ground surrounded on three sides by blocks of flats and playground equipment. There are no reminders of its former use.

Holmes noted that 'This was originally larger than it is now. It was consecrated in 1662 for the parish of St Giles, Cripplegate, and called the pest-house ground. After 1732, when St Luke's parish was formed, it was used by that parish. Now it is neatly laid out and used as a recreation ground by the patients of the St Luke's Asylum.

108. St Luke's Estate is on the site of the former Pest House burial ground.

109. The site of Bath Street pest house is on the left. A green Islington borough plaque on the red brick wall of a modern building reads: CITY PESTHOUSE Built here in open fields 1593. Used during the Great Plague 1665. Demolished 1736. The burial ground is on an estate on the right (see illustration 110).

110. This area of the St Luke's Estate was the pest house burial ground.

111. On the left in Seward Street, behind the railings and now closed up, is a former children's playground which sits on the site of a burial ground used once by St Bartholomew's Hospital for burial of unclaimed bodies. At the bottom of the street to the right is Mount Mills, a 1665 plague pit.

It is ¼ acre in extent.'

There were other burial grounds, also lost, in Bath Street, known in earlier centuries as Pesthouse Row. One belonged to the French Hospital which stood on the site of the Pest House. When the hospital moved in 1866, the bodies were reinterred in the City of London Cemetery.[2]

St Bartholomew's Hospital Ground, Seward Street, EC1

This burial ground may have been used during the 1665 plague, but was, Holmes tells us, for the interment of the unclaimed bodies generated by St Bartholomew's Hospital. The area of burial, about half an acre, was laid out as a public playground in 1891. It is now closed and derelict. It is situated a matter of yards from the Mount Mills plague pit.

112. The St Bartholomew's burial ground behind the railings.

St James Clerkenwell additional ground, Bowling Green Lane, EC1

This burial ground, on the corner of Bowling Green Lane and Clerkenwell Close, was in use between c.1660 and 1853. It is now in the process of being cleared to allow the development of a building for business and residential. The archaeological contractors called in to observe and supervise the exhumations estimated that at least 3000 persons were buried in the cemetery.[3] Holmes described it as:

> ¼ acre in size, situated at the corner of Rosoman Street and Bowling Green Lane. The London School Board secured it when the lease ran out, and it is now the playground of the Bowling Green Lane School.

113. Exhumations at Bowling Green Lane took place behind hoardings. 3000 corpses are thought to have been buried in the ground here.

114. A coffin excavated at Bowling Green Lane .

115. *The coffin of William Jenkins, found beneath Garden Court in the Bank of England in 1933.*

Bank of England, Threadneedle Street, EC2
The graveyard of the old church of St Christopher le Stocks has disappeared, as has the church, which was demolished in 1782. The burial ground was where the Bank of England Garden Court is now. In 1933, when some building work was taking place there, a large lead coffin buried at a depth of 8.5 feet was unearthed bearing the name of William Daniel Jenkins, a former clerk at the Bank who had died in 1798 and fearing body snatchers had asked the Bank's directors if he could be buried in the Bank's grounds. It is presumed that most of the remains from the burial ground were moved to Nunhead Cemetery.

Wesley Chapel ground,City Road, EC1
This ground is an unusual combination of churchyard, office block and recreation ground. Access is opposite the City Road entrance to Bunhill Fields, at the back of Wesley's Chapel, which is worth a visit for the free Museum alone. The ground is tidy with a number of gravestones protruding from concrete underneath the entrance to an office block. The large monument is the site where Wesley and others are buried. Of this ground Holmes in 1896 notedthat it was '½ acre. The part in front of the chapel is neatly kept, but the part behind is closed and not so tidy. Wesley himself was buried in a vault here.[133]

116. *An office block is built over the burial ground at the Wesley Chapel in the City Road.*

117. *The interior of the office block in City Road, which is raised over the burial ground.*

The Friends' burial ground, Bunhill Row, EC1
This ground is located off Bunhill Row, and is not immediately obvious. The Memorial Building mentioned by Holmes is still there, and the remaining portion is now a small park and playground with several memorials. The ground is atmospheric, and peaceful.

Holmes says the ground was 'acquired in 1661, many times added to, and chiefly used by the Friends of the Peel and Bull-and-Mouth divisions. In 1840 a school was built in it. The existing portion is about ½ acre in size, and is neatly kept as a private garden; but the remainder was used as the site for a Board School, a coffee palace, houses and shops, including the Bunhill Fields Memorial Buildings, erected in 1881.'[5]

118. *A plaque in the Friends' burial ground in Bunhill Row which explains its origins.*

119. Entrance to the Friends' burial ground at Bunhill Row.

120. The Golden Lane Campus from Fortune Gardens, where 10,000 bodies were recently exhumed from the area behind the wall.

The City Bunhill (or Golden Lane) burial ground, EC1

This ground lies beneath the new Golden Lane Campus school off Whitecross Street. Nearly 10,000 bodies were exhumed including 30 complete coffins. They were reinterred in the St Pancras and Islington Cemetery in Finchley. The burial ground is identifiable on the 1873 Ordnance Survey map. In March 2008 there was a suggestion in the *Islington Gazette* that the discovery of the exhumed bones might be commemorated either with a glass floor opening on the one-time burial ground, or a display cabinet of artifacts, although no mention is made of what these artifacts might be. Holmes noted that it was a burial ground of '1¼ acres. This was the site of a brewery, and set aside for burials in 1833. About one-third of it is in the City. It is now divided. One part is in the occupation of Messrs. Sutton and Co., carriers, and is full of sheds and carts, the greater part being roofed in, and the southern part has the City mortuary and coroner's court on it. What is unbuilt upon is a neat, private yard between these two buildings. It was closed for burials in 1853.'

Cripplegate Poor-ground, Whitecross Street and Thomas' Golden Lane, EC1

Both of these grounds now lie under the Peabody Estate, no more than 500 yards from the Golden Lane Campus. The Cripplegate Poor-Ground, David Orme suggests, (not shown on Rocque or Horwood), lies under the central open area of the Peabody Estate. Holmes says that 'It was called the 'upper churchyard' of St Giles, and was first used in 1636. 'It was very much overcrowded, the fees being low. A part of the site is occupied by the church and mission-house of St. Mary, Charterhouse, erected in 1864 and only a very small courtyard now exists between these buildings, with a large vault.'

121. The central area of the Peabody Estate, Golden Lane. Two burial grounds are located here.

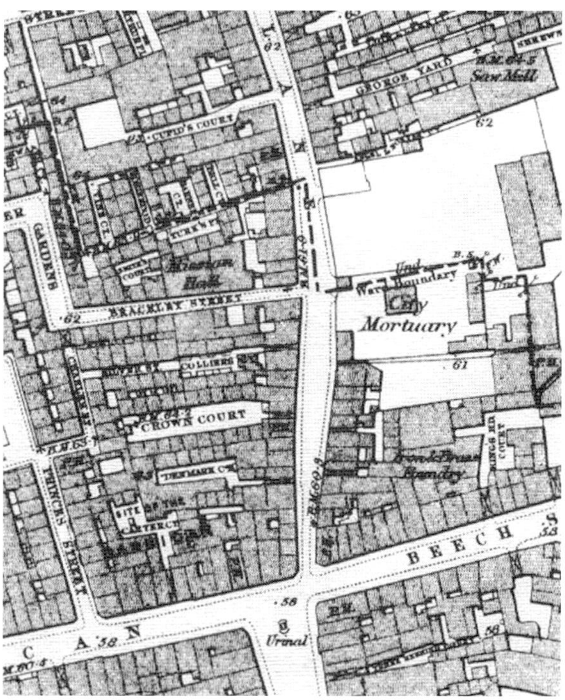

122. The burial ground at Cupid's Court. It is now the Fann Street Wildlife Garden.

123. Map of 1871 showing the Cupid's Court ground to the top.

Cupid's Court Ground, Golden Lane, EC1
This ground can be found by following Brackley Street from Golden Lane until the Fann Street Wildlife Garden appears. It is shown on the 1871 Ordnance Survey map, and then disappears, which may suggest that it lies partly under neighbouring buildings.

124. (Above) The Fann Street Wildlife Garden probably lies on the site of the Cupid's Court burial ground.

125. (Below) Site of the Jones burial ground between Islington Green and Gaskin Street, now developed with apartments.

126. The first Islington Chapel in Gaskin Street.

Islington Chapel-ground, formerly Church Street, now Gaskin Street, N1.

The first Islington Chapel, Methodist, was opened in 1793 in what is now Gaskin Street. In 1800 it was taken over by the Revd Evan Jones who later acquired land at the rear for use as a commercial burial ground. The ground, closed in 1853, lay forgotten in recent years and was mainly used for a timber yard. When it was cleared by commercial contractors in 1996, 1493 coffin plates were recovered.

127. The former Wesleyan chapel in Liverpool Road. The burial ground, described in 1896 as 'containing two tombstones and much rubbish', was beneath the widened road and the bay with the black rubbish bins.

The east side of the ground is now built on, and the west side is a pleasant garden. Holmes says that it was also called Little Bunhill Fields and that 'The original chapel was built in 1788, and had a small graveyard. In 1817 the Rev. Evan Jones bought the garden of 5, Church Row, and added it to this graveyard, the whole ground being nearly 1 acre in extent. It is now in several divisions, part is a yard belonging to the General Post Office, and the other parts are let and sold as builders' yards, or are vacant.[6]

Wesleyan Chapel-ground now Liverpool Road, N1

This burial ground was in front of the old chapel which is now part of the Design Centre to which it is attached. The ground itself is most likely to be the area in front of the buildings where the dustbins in the photograph are located, and partially under the road. Holmes describes it as 'an untidy little closed yard at the west end of the chapel containing two tombstones and much rubbish, and measuring about 225 square yards.'

Maberley Chapel-ground, Ball's Pond Road, N1

Holmes describes this as being about 270 square yards, between the chapel and the road. 'It is closed and bare.'[7] It can be pinpointed as being in front of the newly restored buildings in the car parking area of 47a Ball's Pond Road.

St Martin-in-the-Fields burial-ground in Pratt Street, (now St Martin's Gardens) Camden Town, NW1.

This ground, where an estimated 18,000 burials are recorded, was purchased by St Martin-in-the-Fields in 1805 and remained in use until 1856. Now public gardens, it can be entered either from Camden Street or, more obscurely, behind the now closed St Martin's Tavern in Pratt Street. There are explanatory notices near the entrance, and the large open space still contains many tombstones stacked round the walls, and some table tombs. Immediately behind the tavern is a quiet, overgrown section of burial ground. An addendum in the copy of Holmes' book lent to the author, has in writing: 'Half way

128. Site of the former Maberley chapel ground in Ball's Pond Road. The burial area was between 'the chapel and the road'.

129. St Martin's Gardens in Camden Town, c. 1905, the former St Martin-in-the-Fields burial ground.

130. St Martin's Gardens, Camden Town, today.

down Pratt Street is the St Martin's Tavern, with the churchyard garden of St Martin's on one side ... when the air-raid shelters were being dug, the excavation found so many bodies buried here at the time of the Plague that the work had to be abandoned.' This is, of course, nonsense for the Plague had long since disappeared from London when the ground was opened to ease the pressure on the churchyard of St Martin's at Trafalgar Square. Many bodies were reinterred then in Camden Town when the old churchyard was curtailed for road improvements. This written addendum merely shows just how keen people are to believe that a plague pit exists in their locality.

A principal feature of this ground is a monument to Charles Dibdin, composer of many sea songs such as *Tom Bowling*. He was an ancestor of Lord Michael Heseltine.

Burial ground of Haberdashers' Aske's Hospital and Almshouses, Chart Street, N1

The old burial ground is haunting in its anonymity. It is opposite the old Haberdashers' Aske's hospital building, which eventually became the Haberdashers' Aske's school before its move to Hampstead. The ground was used for the burial of patients as well as others. The ground, shown on the 1872 Ordnance Survey, is situated in the courtyard of a low rise block of flats, on the left, just before Chart Street makes a dog-leg to the right.

West Hackney churchyard, St Paul's church, Stoke Newington Road, N16

The original church was built in the 1820s, but was destroyed during the last war. The present building dates from 1958. The churchyard, long closed, extends some distance behind the church. Access is difficult, and much of the ground is overgrown, with large chest tombs almost completely enveloped by vegetation. The

131. A lost burial ground in Chart Street for Haberdashers' Aske's Hospital (almshouses). The ground is now surrounded by housing blocks.

132. West Hackney churchyard is extensive and overgrown.

133. A 'Danger' sign with an apt skull and crossbones outside the West Hackney churchyard.

churchyard itself is sombre, in places dilapidated.

Holmes says that it was nearly 1½ acres and was consecrated in 1814, and laid out as a public garden in 1885.

Well Street burial ground, St Thomas' Place, E9

Unusually for a disused burial ground, the Well Street ground is well-kept and acknowledged by a large sign. The houses that run parallel to the ground in St Thomas' Place date from 1859.

Holmes notes that this was originally the 'site of the original South Hackney Church. It was laid out as a public garden in 1885, and is very neatly kept by the Hackney District Board of Works. Nearly ¾ acre.'[8]

New Gravel Pit Chapel-ground, Chatham Place, E9

This is one of the more difficult burial grounds to locate. Hidden in a part industrial and part residential area behind high walls and a locked gate, a determined attempt needs to be made to get to it. It is rapidly decaying. The wall fronting the ground on Mead Place is covered by ornamental panels created by local children. A

134. The Well Street burial ground still retains some grave monuments.

135. The old burial ground of the New Gravel Pit chapel, now a fairly derelict area.

notice on the wall placed there by Hackney Council reads, 'These railings were designed with pupils from Morningside School in 1999. They were inspired by the natural beauty of the site and the history of the New Gravel Pit Chapel, which stood on this site from 1810-1970, and its graveyard.'

Holmes wrote about it when the chapel was still open. 'Attached to the Unitarian Church. - ¾ acre. This is full of tombstones and fairly tidy. The gate is usually open, the chapel-keeper living behind the chapel, and having a green-house and fowl-house, &c., in the ground.'[9]

Friends' burial ground, Baker's Row, E1

This ground is now an innocuous East End square, called Vallance Gardens, in Vallance Road, Whitechapel. Holmes noted it as being 'Very nearly an acre. This belonged to the Friends of the Devonshire House division, who acquired it in 1687. It is leased by the society to the Whitechapel District Board of Works, who maintain it as a public recreation ground. It is well laid out and well kept, being chiefly used by children.'[10] The ground was closed in 1857 and still contains a children's playground.

136. The Friends' burial ground in Baker's Row as depicted by Holmes in 1896.

137. Vallance Gardens, the site of the Quaker burial ground formerly known as Baker's Row.

East London Cemetery, Shandy Street, E1
In the vicinity of St Dunstan's, Stepney is the site of the former Shandy Street burial ground. This was a private ground opened around 1830 and was also known as the Beaumont burial ground. Holmes describes it as 'much crowded'. It was made into a playground and public garden in 1885. It includes the remains of St Faith's church, built in 1891, mostly destroyed during the last war.

Aldgate burial ground, Cartwright Street, Royal Mint Square, E1
This ground is just off East Smithfield near the Royal Mint. The road, apart from the 'recreation ground', is completely residential and there is no indication that the open grassy area is actually a former burial place. It belonged to the parish of St Botolph, Aldgate and was consecrated in 1615. Holmes tells us that at the beginning of the 19th century 'it was covered with small houses, the Weigh House School being built on it in 1846. The rookery was cleared by the Metropolitan Board of Works, and Darby Street was made, gravestones and remains being then discovered. The Metropolitan Public Gardens Association informed the Board of the former existence of a burial-ground, with the result that what remained of the burial-ground was not built upon, but was made into an asphalted playground, about 1 acre in extent, for the children of the adjoining block of tenements. [11]

The area was excavated by the Museum of London in 2005 during the course of some redevelopment. 238 burials were unearthed of which 28 were left on site. Interestingly, this was only a part of the burial ground, suggesting that a large part of the ground still remains to be found. Most of the graves contained more than two burials with some containing four or five. The archaeologists suggest that the nature of some of the burials, and the fact that the burial ground dates from the first part of the 17th century, makes it 'a likely contender for use for mass burials, or that graves were continually being reused as space became a premium in the later years of the graveyard.'[12]

138 and 139. Two views of the Shandy Street burial ground site. Note the remains in the the top illustration of the 1891 St Faith's church, which was bombed during the last war.

140. Site of the St Botolph, Aldgate burial ground in Cartwright Street, Royal Mint Square. It was due to be developed in the 19th century, but the discovery of bones led to it being asphalted for recreation.

St Katharine's Dock, next to Tower Bridge, E1
The area now occupied by shops, flats and the marina once contained two large burial grounds. Today, nothing remains of them.

Holmes records that 'when St. Katharine's Docks were made, in 1827, St Katharine's church, the ruins of the hospital (dating from 1148), two churchyards of considerable size, and the whole parish, – inns, streets, houses and all, were totally annihilated ... It is said that a quantity of the human remains from the churchyard were used to fill up some old reservoirs, &c., in the neighbourhood; but at any rate, it is a fact that they were distributed amongst the East-end churchyards, and several cartloads were taken to Bethnal Green and deposited in St Matthew's ground where the slope up to the west door of the church is composed of these bodies from St Katharine's. There were originally steps leading to the entrance, but the steps are buried under this artificial hill, the ground having been raised several inches.'[13]

141. Rocque's map of 1746 showing the two burial grounds of St Katharine's Hospital precinct.

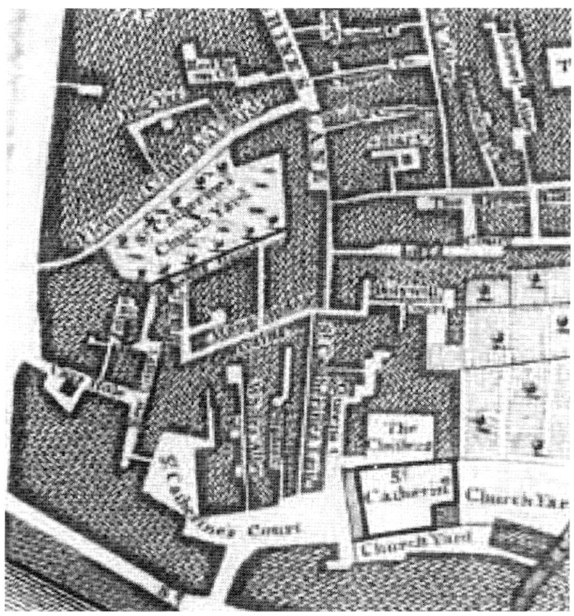

142. St Katharine's dock, itself now displaced, covered the site of two former churchyards attached to the St Katharine's precinct just outside the walls of the Tower of London. When the dock was built in 1827 cartloads of human remains were taken away and many were reinterred at the nearby St Matthew's, Bethnal Green, where the results can still be seen.

Bancroft Almshouses, Mile End Road, E1

Holmes comments that one of the most interesting almshouse burial grounds 'is one which belonged to the Bancroft Almshouses in Mile End Road. The fate of the asylum itself is well known; it has been replaced by the People's Palace, and the improvement from an antiquarian or architectural point of view is nil ... The graveyard of Bancroft's Almshouses was a long strip on the eastern side. Part of it has been merged into the roadway. St Benet's Church Hall, and the Vicarage were built upon it, and the bones of the pensioners are under the Vicarage garden.' She continues to describe a part of the burial ground, that with a little searching in the forecourt of Queen Mary's College, is still visible:

143. A relic of the Bancroft Almshouses, at the western edge of the Queen Mary College fronting Mile End Road.

The northernmost point of the graveyard is enclosed and roofed over, and forms a little yard where flag-

144. Bancroft's Almshouses and School, Mile End Road, founded in 1727 and administered by the Drapers' Company. The buildings were demolished c. 1884 to be replaced by the People's Palace.

staffs, &c., are stored. But between this and the wall of the Vicarage there is a piece open to the road, with some heaps of stone in it and rubbish. There are, at any rate, four gravestones left, against the wall, and there may be others behind the stones; but I daresay it is only a very small proportion of those who pass in and out of the Palace who have ever noticed this relic of the Bancroft Almshouses.[14]

Shoreditch burial ground, (Hackney Road Recreation Ground) Hackney Road, E2

This burial ground is easy to miss. Situated on Hackney Road approximately 300 yards east of Shoreditch church, it is next door to a public house, and is partly covered by a derelict tennis court. There are a few remaining tombstones next to the pavement. Recent work on the buildings adjoining the ground yielded quantities of human bones. Holmes describes it as being of ½ acre. She also mentioned that 'this has an ancient watch-house in it, which was subsequently used as a cholera hospital. In 1891 the Metropolitan Public Gardens Association laid it out as a public playground, and it is maintained by the Burial Board.' Of the watch-house and cholera hospital nothing remains.

St Matthew's, St Matthew's Row, off Bethnal Green Road, E2

St Matthew's is an imposing church with a large well looked-after churchyard. Holmes says of this church that 'In Bethnal Green, for instance, not only is there the burial-ground of St Matthew's, which was consecrated in 1746, and has vaults under the school as well as the church...'[15]

By 1819 the ground was full, and burials were extended by using vaults under the new National school which had been built on part of the churchyard and was completed in 1820. There were 17 vaults, each capable of holding 20 bodies.

'In 1826 the vestry stopped the bringing of 'boxes or cases of bones' from St. Katharine's and other London churches to St Matthew's churchyard, where *c.* 50,000 had been buried by 1848. Burials in St Matthew's churchyard and vaults were discontinued from 1853. ...'

145. The former St Leonard's Shoreditch burial ground in Hackney Road. The site also includes a derelict tennis court which is on top of some of the ground.

Hector Gavin wrote in 1848 that:

... in St Matthew's the ground has been very considerably raised by the numerous bodies which have been interred. I regret to state, that at no very great distance of time it was the practice to burn the coffins in one of the church-yards; it would be needless to inquire what became of the corpses ... It is the practice in St Matthew's to bury in vaults, in the church, and as lately as last week a body was thus deposited. This practice is most abominable and reprehensible, and imperiously demands immediate abatement, as an offensive, dangerous, and disgusting nuisance. The smells and exhalations from a dead body are quite as offensive, and deleterious, as those from a dead ox or horse.[16]

He continued:

The better to illustrate the necessity of supervision, to improve the sanitary condition of schools, those attached to St Matthews and St James-the-Less may be selected. The St Matthew schools, consist of the Charity, National, and Infant Schools, they were built in 1846, and consist of two large rooms, for scholastic purposes; there are other rooms, for other purposes. The building is situate in the north western corner of the church-yard, which is filled to repletion with corpses, the underground portion of the building consists of a central passage 49 feet long, and a side entrance. This passage is branched with seventeen brick vaults, or low cellars, which are used as catacombs, four of these are public cellars, in these last I counted ninety-six coffins piled one on the other, like so many bales of goods. I could not ascertain the number of bodies deposited in the other vaults, one only of which was bricked up. There is a large aperture at the end of the passage, for the emission of air from this place, the aperture is right under, and close to, the back entrance to the school, as well as to a most abominably filthy privy used by the children. On endeavouring to examine the state of this place, I was overcome by the most distressing nausea I have ever experienced during my sanitary investigations; whether this nausea

146. *St Matthew's Bethnal Green. The slope is from the build up of bodies buried beneath the step and surrounding area which were reinterred here from St Katharine's precinct near the Tower of London when St Katharine's Dock was constructed.*

147. *St Matthew's burial ground, showing the old watch house in the corner and a modern version of the old school which stood at the bottom of the burial ground.*

should be entirely attributed to the filthy cesspool, or was partly due to the escape of foul air from the catacombs, I did not stay to inquire. I presume, however, that it was chiefly attributable to the former cause. How the children can use, and remain in, such a place, is almost incomprehensible.'[17]

St George-in-the-East churchyard, Cannon Street Road, E1

The church now doubles as a Montessori School. The crypt was described by Walker in 1839 as 'greatly crowded, and in a loathsome state.' Next to the memorial on the road side of the churchyard is an old semi-derelict building which was a mortuary. The north side of the churchyard is in 2008 being cleared and made into an open space. Holmes tells us that the ground, which dates from about 1730, was once two grounds, the wall of which was taken down in 1875. The remains of the wall can still be seen. She describes the grounds which were laid out as public gardens as 'beautifully kept. The size of the whole garden, consisting of the two graveyards, is about 3 acres.'

148. The St George-in-the-East churchyard in Cannon Street Road. The ruined building behind the tree is an old mortuary.

1 George A. Walker, *Gatherings from Grave Yards* (1839), p.183

2 Info. ex David Orme

3 See http://www.aocarchaeology.com/bowlinggreen.htm.

4 John Stow, *Survey of London* (1598, 1840 edn), p.170.

5 Isabella (Mrs Basil) Holmes, *The London Burial Grounds* (1896), p.291

6 *Ibid*, p.290.

7 *Ibid*, p.290

8 *Ibid*, p.293.

9 *Ibid*, p.293

10 *Ibid*, p.297

11 *Ibid*, p.296

12 Royal Mint Square, El. MoLAS (Bruce Ferguson) excavation and watching brief October-December 2005, London Borough of Tower Hamlets RM105.

13 Holmes, p.115.

14 *Ibid*, pp.180-1.

15 *Ibid*, p.111.

16 Hector Gavin, *Sanitary Ramblings, being Sketches and Illustrations of Bethnal Green* (1848), pp.72-3

17 Gavin, p.85.

CHAPTER SIX

SOUTHWARK

It was not the intention in this book to cover the numerous and often interesting lost and forgotten burial grounds south of the Thames, but many deserve comment, one in particular, the Cross Bones ground. This ground in 2008 is the centre of a development controversy that may well lead to its destruction.

Bermondsey Abbey, Abbey Street

Not included in either Walker or Holmes, this burial ground is on the site of the 11th-century Bermondsey Abbey, a Cluniac monastery, which when excavated between 1984 and 1986 by the Museum of London yielded 200 skeletons. (Nearby is the Cluny housing estate.) The ground is marked by a blue hoarding almost opposite

150. Behind the hoarding are the remains of the Abbey and part of its cemetery.

149. The remains of Bermondsey Abbey 1805, showing its burial ground in the foreground. Drawing by C J Whichelo.

the church of St Mary Magdalene, and is situated on the corner of two roads, Abbey Street and Long Walk, SE1.

St Saviour's Additional ground known as 'Cross Bones.' Redcross Way, SE1

This ground in Redcross Way, near the railway line which cuts through the area, would be inconspicuous were it not for the many ribbons and notes attached to the gate beyond which the now obliterated burial ground lies. The site is derelict and belongs to Transport for London. It holds the remains of many of London's early paupers and prostitutes, and has been the subject of a number of controversial development applications. It is thought the ground still holds the remains of about 15,000 bodies, in unmarked silence, buried just below the concrete surface of a car park.

Some remains have been disturbed during periodic building work, especially in the 1920s and again in the 1990s when the Jubilee Line was extended. There is at present a vociferous local campaign to turn the ground into an open space, whilst the owners have appealed against a refusal to allow them to build on the site.

Planning disagreements are not new in relation to this site for in 1896 Holmes wrote of this small, desolate area:

This was made, at least 250 years ago, 'far from the parish church', for the interment of the low women who frequented the neighbourhood. It was subsequently used as the pauper ground, and was crowded to excess. Nevertheless two schools were built in it. The remaining piece is about 1,000 square yards, It has frequently been offered for sale as a building site, and has formed the subject for much litigation. It is made partial use of by being let for fairs, swings, &c. It was sold as a building site in 1883, but, not having been used by 1884, the sale was declared (under the Disused Burial Grounds Act) null and void.

151. A poster and ribbons put up by local residents in response to an application to develop the site of the old burial ground.

Inevitably, George Walker in 1839 included the overcrowded state of this ground in his *Gatherings from Grave Yards*:

The poor ground, called 'Cross Bones', in Red Cross Street, Union Street, Borough, also belongs to this parish. The greater portion of this ground has not been opened for some time past, in consequence of its very crowded state; the remaining part, however, is still used for interments, many of the poor Irish are buried in it. Two charity schools, one for boys and the other for girls, are built at the west end, in Union Street, the back parts of which run into this ground. On the 20th February last, a vestry meeting was holden 'for the purpose of considering the propriety of re-opening the Cross Bones burying ground'. The ground had been closed about two years (the time generally

152. The burial ground is behind the hoarding on the right. There are no traces of burials.

153. Layers of bones at the Cross Bones burial ground. (From the MoLAS publication, The Cross Bones Burial Ground.)

allowed for the destruction of the bodies!) and it was moved that it be re-opened; the mover of the resolution stating, that in consequence of the aversion generally manifested to bury in what is named the 'Irish corner', many bodies were taken out of the parish to be buried. This corner, however, had been cleared, and room made for about a thousand bodies. One gentleman argued that 'if the graves had been made deeper, hundreds more corpses might have been buried there.' Another admitted that it really was too bad to bury within eighteen inches of the surface, in such a crowded neighbourhood; and it was even hinted that 'the clearing', viz. the digging up and the removal of the decayed fragments of flesh and bones, with the pieces of coffin, &c. would be the best course, were it not for the additional expense. The fund of the vestry and the health of the living were here placed in opposite scales: the former had its preponderance.'[1]

It had been found in 1832 that the ground was very full of coffins and that it was necessary to bury within two feet of the surface. '...the effluvium is so very offensive that we fear the consequences may be very injurious to the surrounding neighbourhood.' Closure of the ground was urged.[2]

However, the ground remained open. A further attempt to have it closed took place in August 1845 when Mariane Gwilt who lived nearby at the school house in Union Street, complained to the Board of Health, painting an unsettling picture of the state of the ground:

From the windows of the room called the School room we have all this sickly Summer almost daily witnessed the most distressing sights; our remonstrances are vain – in the bone house with its open grating which is not more than eight or ten yards

154. A shrine to the Virgin Mary has been placed in the yard.

from five of our windows we have during these last fatal six weeks had sometimes as many as from three to nine bodies lying in their shells [coffins] at a time for days (as many as ten days) in the aforesaid Bone house close under our windows, - One of these shells contained the body of a woman who was brought here supposed dead from Cholera, but actually broke a blood vessel, trying to get out, whilst being carried along she not being dead then - The saw dust and shavings saturated with blood which washed out the shell when the body was transferred into the permanent Coffin was spread under our windows and is there now although this occurred three weeks ago. On another occasion three or four weeks since the body of a man who had drowned himself at Blackfriars Bridge was brought down here and allowed to lie in its shell ten days when the body was washed with a mop and pailsful of water and the shell again washed out and all the filthy liquid and shavings and grass thrown under our windows his clothes lie there at this time I am writing and whilst he lay'd there the bodies of two children who had died of the Cholera was left in this dead house the chief of the time ... Our kitchen on the ground floor with the School room over it forms the wing which looks into this burial ground - the earth of which comes at least four feet above the level of the said kitchen floor owing to the number of burials which take place and it is now rendered very damp and unhealthy....[3]

The Board of Health denied Gwilt's claims, and the ground stayed open. In November 1852 local inhabitants made further representations, which included a graphic account of practices:

... the Gravedigger is daily seen with a long steel pointed Iron Rod sticking the ground here and there spearing the top coffins, until some wood gives way, whereupon the whole of the contents, however manifold the coffins may be 'sometimes many' in that particular Grave are turned out and remain several days above ground to the scandal of all Christian men. When each of these exhumations have taken place there have been seen and repeatedly counted in different lots of such human remains a number of skulls too numerous lying like half devoured Turnips about a Sheepfold and cared for as little...[4]

The graveyard was finally closed in 1853, on the grounds that it was 'completely overcharged with dead' and that further burials would be 'inconsistent with a due regard for the public health and public decency'. In 1883, it was sold as a building site, prompting Lord Brabazon to write to *The Times:*

'... with a view to save this ground from such desecration, and to retain it as an open space for the use and enjoyment of the people.'

In 1928 some bones were disturbed during building work. A newspaper of the day noted that 40 skeletons were found, though many others remained elsewhere.[5] These were placed in coffins and reburied at Brookwood Cemetery. The following year the sale of the ground was declared null and void under the Disused Burial Grounds Act (1884). Subsequent attempts to develop the site were fiercely resisted by local people. The land was briefly used as a fair-ground.

The present 'Friends of Cross Bones' state succinctly the cause of their campaign is the peaceful recognition of the site as a burial ground. They claim that Museum of London archaeologists had removed some 148 skeletons in the 1990s, though they had estimated this was less than 1% of the number of burials there. In 2002, Southwark Council refused planning permission for three office-blocks to be erected on the graveyard. However the decision was overturned on appeal, which means that Transport for London now have permission to develop the site. Obviously, its commercial value means that some development is inevitable, but unless this is sensitive it risks desecrating the past and arousing the opposition of present-day residents.

The Friends are proposing that an area (between the Redcross Way gate and the junction with Union Square) should be a Cross Bones memorial park. This might be only a small plot of land, with a tree and a tombstone – perhaps bearing the inscription: 'The Outcast Dead' – with a brief account of the history of this paupers' graveyard.'[6]

Deadman's Place burial ground, Park Street, SE1

This burial ground, which dates from the 16th century, was used for plague victims. It is now occupied by the car parks of the Novotel and the Southwark Rose Hotel. There is nothing to indicate its former function.

The ground later became the graveyard of an adjoining Independent chapel, and was extensively used for the interment of ministers, being a sort of Bunhill Fields for south London.

155. Deadman's Place, one of the more unusual burial grounds, lies beneath the car park of Southwark Novotel. Walker in 1839 said that it was 'surcharged with dead'.

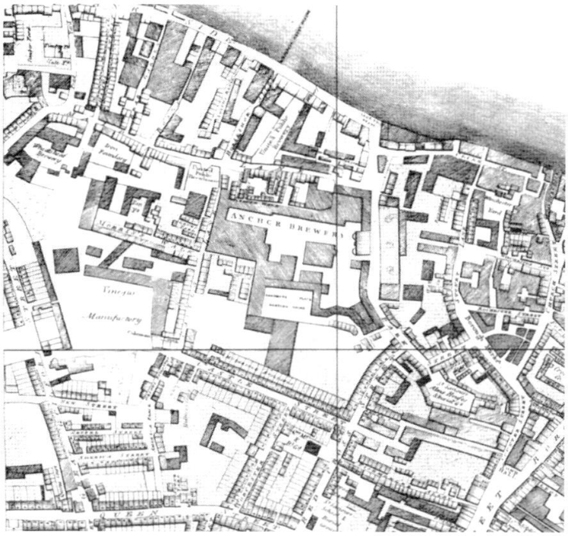

156. *Horwood's map of 1799 shows the Deadman Place burial gound in the centre of this detail, south of the Anchor Brewery.*

'Now it is merely one of the yards over which trucks run on rails, in the middle of the large brewery belonging to Messrs. Barclay and Perkins, about ½ acre in extent. It existed as a burial-ground in 1839, but not, I believe, in 1843.'[7]

Ewer Street chapel and burial ground, SE1

There is little to see of this burial ground in Ewer Street, about 500 yards from where it joins Union Street. It lies immediately alongside the railway into Charing Cross. The blue gate in the centre of the illustration marks the entrance to the site.

Walker says of this ground:

EWER STREET CHAPEL AND BURYING GROUND, at the bottom of Union Street, Borough.– The burying ground appears to have been raised nearly six feet from the original surface, and is literally surcharged with dead; it is now closed, and presents a very repulsive aspect. It might be instructive to know the number of bodies here inhumed; perhaps, – but dead men tell no tales, – the exhumed might present a formidable array. The vicinity is disgustingly dirty.[8]

Remains were removed *c.* 1861 when the railway to Charing Cross was built, though judging by recent finds many were left *in situ*. The SE1 community website comments:

... this is the site of an unmarked graveyard, as discovered in about 1990 [actually June 1987] by some workmen who were renewing the concrete floor

157. *Ewer Street burial ground is on the right. In 1839 Walker said that it was '... now closed and presents a very repulsive aspect'.*

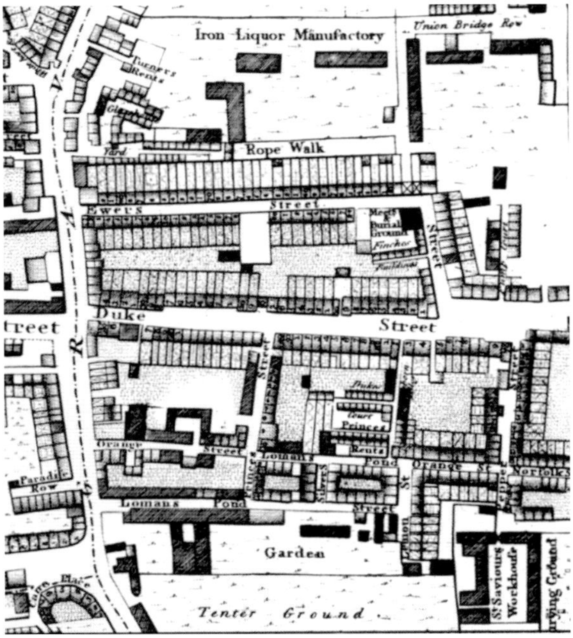

158. Ewer Street chapel and its burial ground are tucked into the dog-leg of Ewer Street. Shown here on Horwood's map of 1799.

under two of the railway arches when they came across a skull. Suspecting foul play, the police were called in. The police called in a pathologist. He called in an archaeologist ... about 200 skeletons were eventually unearthed and dated to some time after the Black Death but before WWII ... the bones were reburied elsewhere (but only two of the arches were excavated). It appears that when the viaduct was built the contractors came across the graveyard, said nothing and moved the graves which were in the way of the piers, resulting in a lot of the bodies being reburied standing up and bones just jumbled up together very close to the surface.'[9]

Additional ground for St Saviour's, called the College Yard or St Saviour's Almshouse burial ground, Park Street, SE1

This ground came into use around 1730 and was purchased in 1860 by a railway company, when railway arches were built over the ground. Human remains were uncovered and moved to both Brookwood cemetery in Woking and Nunhead cemetery. The rest of the ground was

159. The College Yard burial ground in Park Street during the first half of the 19th century.

160. *The College Yard or St Saviour's Almshouse burial ground is now beneath the railway.*

used as a builder's yard and is now part of Borough Market. Holmes says that it 'existed before 1732. Size, $\frac{1}{4}$ acre. The London, Brighton and South Coast Railway goes over it on arches, and it is now the storeyard of Messrs. Stone and Humphries, builders. Most of it is roofed in but it is not actually covered with buildings.'

Baptist burial ground, (Bandy Leg Walk) now Southwark Bridge Road
St Saviour's Workhouse ground, SE1

There is no indication that the area of the Victorian fire station and the next door Fire Museum on this busy road was once the site of a burial ground. Skeletons were unearthed during construction work on the station in 1884. The site, originally part of the unsuccessful Grotto Gardens Pleasure Ground founded in 1760, is now lost under Southwark Bridge Road.

Holmes noted: 'In 1807 there existed the St Saviour's Workhouse, with a burial ground on the east side of it which, from its position, may have coincided with the Baptists' ground, and what is now left of the burial-ground is a garden or courtyard, about 1,000 square yards in size, between the new buildings of the Central Fire Brigade Station in Southwark Bridge Road, and the old house behind them. It is entered through the large archway.'

In 1988 skeletons were found when laying pipes in the fire station car park. The workhouse ground was adjacent and to the east of the Baptist ground. It was formed in 1777 as a poor ground.[10]

161. *The site of the Baptist burial ground in Southwark Bridge Road. In 1988 skeletons were found when laying pipes in the fire station car park.*

162. Site of a Quaker burial ground in O'Meara Street, in use from at least 1666. The construction of the railway destroyed the ground and 9 bodies were also found on this site during work on the Jubilee Line Extension in 1994.

Friends' burial-ground, O'Meara Street, SE1

The car park next to the Charing Cross railway arch is the site of a Quaker burial ground which was in use by 1666. There was a Friends' Meeting House to the south of O'Meara Street (formerly Worcester Street) which had its own burial ground. This was built in 1674. The ground was full by 1733 and its level was raised to allow more burials. The ground closed in 1794, and in 1860 the land was compulsorily purchased by the Metropolitan Board of Works to build Southwark Street. The ground was destroyed the same year when the railway was constructed. The Friends supervised the clearing of the ground. A report of the exhumations then states that, 'with the exception of lead coffins in various states of preservation, the remains were found to have become reduced to skeletons; and although there was a considerable amount of loose coffin wood ... no bodies were found nearer the surface than seven feet, showing the care Friends had taken not to overcrowd the ground ... [the remains] were all removed (by hearse) at various times to the burial-ground at Long Lane, Bermondsey.'[11] The report goes on to observe that 956 remains were exhumed. A number of lead coffins were found, and opened to see the state of preservation of the corpses – the conclusion being that in general, burial in lead did little to halt decomposition. The exhumations by no means included the total number interred. In October 1994, 9 bodies were found here during work on the Jubilee Line Extension at the corner of Southwark Street and O'Meara Street.[12]

1 George A. Walker, *Gatherings from Grave Yards* (1839), pp.177-8.
2 *The Cross Bones Burial Ground* (Museum of London), p.9.
3 *Ibid*, p.12.
4 *Ibid*, p.15.
5 *Ibid*, p.19.
6 http://www.southwark.co.uk/SouthwarkDiscussion/ShowPost.aspx?PostID=1063.
7 Isabella (Mrs Basil) Holmes, *The London Burial Grounds* (1896), p.309.
8 Walker, p.179.
9 Ex SE1 community website forum 2002.
10 Info ex David Orme.
11 *Cross Bones*, pp.49-51.
12 O'Meara Street car parks grouting shaft, SE1 TQ3239 8012 MoLAS (Aidan Woodger) excavation Oct. 1994, London Underground Ltd OMS94.

CHAPTER SEVEN

JEWISH BURIAL GROUNDS

The Jewish population of England is small; now fewer than 200,000. Jews were here by the time of the Norman Conquest, but were expelled by Edward I in 1290 and not permitted to return until 1656. Mrs Holmes refers to a number of areas which were used for their burial. Prior to the year 1177, there was only one place that Jews were allowed to be buried:

It was known as the Jews' Garden and was outside the wall of London by Cripplegate, several acres being devoted to the purpose – a neighbourhood subsequently known by the name of Leyrestowe. When other burial-places were permitted, this ground was built upon, but the remembrance of it still lives in the name of one street in the district, Jewin Street, reminding us of the time of the bitter persecutions which the Jews suffered ...[1]

Jewin Street, or 'Jewen' on the Rocque map of 1746, is just to the east of the Barbican off Aldersgate Street. Holmes observed that its very size and position made it inevitable that it would disappear under new streets as London grew.

Jewish burial ground, Fulham Road

This ground fronts the Fulham Road and is anonymous to the passer-by. Behind a black locked door, and invisible from the street, lies a cemetery, overlooked by the nearby flats. Of this

163. A disused Jewish cemetery hidden behind a wall in the Fulham Road.

164. The locked entrance to the disused Jewish 'Western Cemetery' in Fulham Road (2008).

former mulberry orchard Holmes said that it was half an acre and 'belongs to the Western Synagogue, St. Alban's Place, S. W., and was first used in 1813. It is closed to the public except between 11 and 4 on Sundays'.[2] Without knowledge of its location, finding this ground would be bordering on the impossible, unless one lives in one of the overlooking flats.

Jewish burial ground, Kingsbury Road, off Ball's Pond Road, N16

The ground is a short distance from the Ball's Pond Road on the edge of a low-rise estate. The original wall is the only indication of this long disused cemetery. Holmes wrote that it was '1¼ acres. This belongs to the West London Synagogue, is very neatly kept, and is still in use. It is full of very large tombstones.'[3]

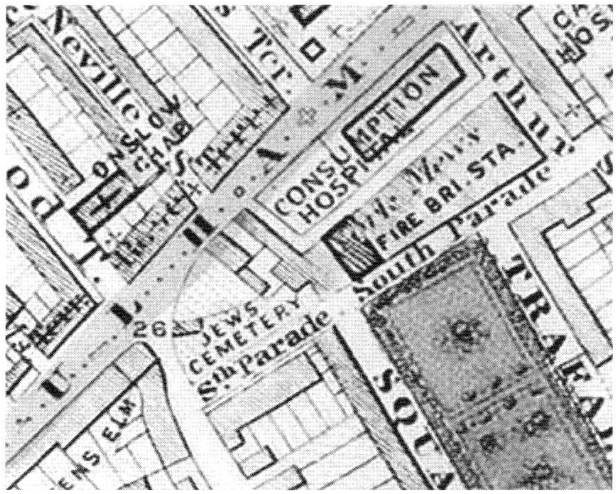

165. The location of the Jewish Cemetery in the Fulham Road.

166. The locked and chained entrance to the Kingsbury Road cemetery.

Jewish burial ground, Lauriston Road, formerly Grove Street, E9

The cemetery is a prominent feature in Lauriston Road. It was in use by 1788 and until the closure of the Hambro Synagogue in London in 1892. The cemetery is closed but is still recognizable from Holmes' brief description: '2¼ acres. This belongs to the United Synagogue, and was purchased in 1788. It is closed and full of erect tombstones, and has some trees and flower-beds near the entrance.

167. The 19th-century Jewish burial ground in Kingsbury Road is desolate, with dangerous areas sealed off with tape.

168. In use since at least 1788, this Jewish cemetery in Lauriston Road has survived relatively unscathed. It was closed in 1892.

169. The southern end of the Lauriston Road cemetery is the most atmospheric.

Alderney Road cemetery, Stepney, E1.
This is a little-known cemetery near Stepney Green underground station. It was the first Ashkenasi burial ground in England formed after the Resettlement of 1656.

Benjamin Levy, acting from the highest motives of disinterest, for his own burial rights were secure, bought from Captain Nathaniel Owen a plot of garden-land contiguous to the Sephardi cemetery in Mile End on 2 February 1696 (Old Style) or 2 February 1697 (New Style) on a lease for 999 years, at a peppercorn rent, for £190.

By the middle of the eighteenth century it was necessary to purchase a further plot immediately adjacent. This was in Three Colt Yard which subsequently became Colt Yard and eventually, the present name.

The ground opened around 1697 and was extended in 1749. It closed in 1852.[4]

The Rocque map shows that Three Colt Yard is some hundred yards to the west of the Mile End Road cemetery which is shown as the 'Jews Old Burying Ground.' Holmes describes it as being '... nearly five acres in extent and still in use, just beyond the People's Palace.'

The Alderney Road cemetery was guarded against 'resurrection men'.

A feature of the Cemetery in the old days was a sort of wheeled sentry-box, which was moved about the ground and from which new graves were watched for some nights after a burial had taken place, as a precaution against the activities of the so-called 'Resurrection men' who supplied Medical Schools with corpses for dissection. Members of the Congregation, in pairs and armed with blunderbusses, took turns to perform this cold and rather gruesome duty, and in the records of the Synagogue there are preserved rosters of the roll of duty 'for the guarding of the House of Life'.[5]

170. Alderney Road Jewish burial ground. Originally opened in 1697, it was extended in 1749. It is now a large, fully enclosed garden. Permission for entry is required.

171. This tomb in Alderney Road is unusual in a Jewish cemetery, in that it has a prominent skull motif.

172. The two Rothschild tombs in Brady Street cemetery mentioned by Holmes are guarded by railings. The tomb on the left is that of Nathaniel Victor Mayer Rothschild who was buried here in 1990.

173. Brady Street cemetery, showing the raised centre section for double burials where 'foreigners' or non-local Jews were buried.

Brady Street, E1

Brady Street (formerly North Street) cemetery lies behind a wall protected by broken glass, a little way past Mocatta House on the left when approached from the Brady Street junction with Whitechapel Road. An area of wall can be peered over, but entry requires an appointment made with the United Synagogue burial authority. The cemetery, which opened in 1761, is unusual in that when it filled up, a raised area in the centre was created for 'foreigners'. The headstones in this area lie back to back. Holmes wrote:

...there are walls running through it, and the southern half is higher than the northern half, having quite a hilly appearance. The following is the explanation. This half of the ground was originally allotted to 'strangers', Jews who belonged to no special congregation. About thirty years after it was full, a layer of earth, 4 feet in depth, was added to the ground, and it was used over again. As the coffins were again placed 6 feet from the surface, there still remained 4 feet of earth between them and the old ones beneath. As a result of this curious and interesting arrangement, there may be seen, in several cases, two gravestones standing up back to back, which represent the two graves below them.[6]

Three interesting tombs are those of Nathan Mayer Rothschild, his wife Hannah and Nathaniel Mayer Rothschild, the third Baron Rothschild. Nathan died in 1836, and Nathaniel in 1990. The latter decided he would be buried next to his ancestors to prevent the local council from placing a compulsory purchase order on the site. His burial meant that the ground was safe from development for another 100 years.

In 1665 the great plague devastated London and the Jewish community suffered heavily. It is known that at least 6 victims of the plague were buried in what

174. Bancroft Road Jewish cemetery. First used in 1811, by 1884 it had fallen into a state of disrepair and by 1895 it was practically filled up. Today it is crumbling and neglected.

was then the new cemetery in Mile End Road. Another cemetery was opened in 1791. In 1811 observant German Jewish immigrants dissatisfied with the Great Synagogue in Dukes Place formed the 'New Synagogue' in Leadenhall Street in the City. In that time it was incumbent upon every synagogue to provide its own burial grounds and the 'New' leased this place at 12 guineas per annum as a cemetery. So this cemetery is the third oldest and largest for its time. (It must be remembered that United Synagogues comprising the 'Great', the 'New' and Hambro was only formed in 1870 and shared burial grounds) ...

The cemetery closed in 1858 except for reserved graves.'[7]

Bancroft Road, Tower Hamlets, E1

The Bancroft Road Jewish cemetery came into use in 1811, and by 1884 it was observed by the *Jewish Chronicle* to be in a state of disrepair. It is described by Holmes as 'another dreary place, which, although in so crowded a district, is still in use.' Today the cemetery is vandalised with few gravestones still standing. It was bombed during the last war and evidence of damage can still be seen. Many of the tombstones lie flat with jagged scars.

175. Entrance to the Old Velho Sephardi cemetery in Mile End Road.

Old Velho Sephardi cemetery behind Albert Stern House at 253 Mile End Road, E1

This cemetery lies directly behind No. 253 Mile End Road. The immediate surroundings are a remnant of Victorian London. The entrance is by way of a small archway, and access to the graveyard is by prior appointment. Some careful peeking over a wall, bearing in mind the various health and safety aspects, will allow a panoramic view of the ground, which essentially remains the same as in Mrs Holmes' 1896 photograph.

There is a plaque on the front of Albert Stern House which states:

...Behind this building lies the first cemetery of the Spanish and Portuguese Jews who fled from the persecutions of the Spanish and Portuguese Inquisition to find religious toleration and freedom in this realm.

They founded in the City of London in 1650 the congregation called Shaar HaShamayim – The Gate of Heaven – which is still in existence. It was the first professing Jewish community in the British Isles established in Modern times and formed the origin of the present Jewish community of Britain as a whole.

176. The Old Velho cemetery as photographed for Mrs Holmes in 1896.

177. The Old Velho cemetery in 2008. Albert Stern House is on the left.

178. The Novo Beth Chaim Sephardi cemetery on the Queen Mary College Campus, Mile End Road.

Novo Beth Chaim Sephardi cemetery, Queen Mary College campus, Mile End Road, E1

This cemetery was opened in 1725 and closed in the 1920s. Viewing it requires entry to the Queen Mary's College campus and the cemetery is near the Faculty of Arts building and easily accessible. It lies on the eastern side, providing a contrast to the vibrant daily campus life nearby. The cemetery was partly built over when the campus expanded in the 1970s with the remains of some 7500 deceased being exhumed. Around 2000 graves remain.[8]

1 Isabella (Mrs Basil) Holmes, *The London Burial Grounds* (1896), p.155

2 *Ibid*, p.283

3 *Ibid*, p.290

4 *Ibid*, p.159

5 See www.jewisheastend.com

6 Holmes, p.157

7 See www.jewisheastend.com

8 I am grateful to Philip Walker, and his marvellous website (www.jewisheastend.com), for much of the information relating to the Jewish cemeteries, though I have visited them all myself.

APPENDIX

A list of London burial grounds taken from Edwin Chadwick's *A special inquiry into the practice on interments in towns* (1843).

PLACES OF BURIAL.	Population in 1841.	Estimated Extent in Square Yards.	Annual Number of Burials.	No. of Burials per Acre.
Allhallows Barking, Great Tower Street	1,924	825	50	293
Allhallows, Bread Street	263	100	'Scarcely any'	..
Allhallows, Lombard Street	516	350	'Seldom used.'	..
Allhallows, London Wall	1,620	615	24	189
Allhallows, Staining Lane	502	619	20	156
Allhallows-the-Great, Thames Street	672	346	50	319
Allhallows-the-Less, ditto	181	412		
Alphage, St. London Wall	976	388	50	624
Andrew's, St.	35,301	4,840	250	250
Andrew's, St. Burial-ground, Gray's Inn Lane	..	9,258	312	163
Andrew's, St. Undershaft	1,163	265	70	1,278
Andrew's, St. Wardrobe, and St. Ann, Blackfriars	3,596	657	100	737
Anne, St. and St. Agnes within Aldersgate	513	1,650	70	205
Ann's, St. Limehouse	19,337	24,500	150	30
Anne's, St. Soho	16,480	2,732	200	354
Augustine's, St. and St. Faith's	1,070	3,700	30	39
Bartholomew, St. the Great	3,414	783	100	618
Bartholomew, St. the Less	744	183	8	212
Benet, St. Fink	383	277	6	105
Benet, St. Paul's Wharf	588	297	36	587
Bennet, St. Sherehog	145	145	'Seldom used.'	..
Botolph, St. Aldersgate	5,906	1,918	250	631
Botolph, St. Aldgate	9,525	1,545	250	783
Botolph, St. Bishopsgate	10,969	3,034	250	399
Botolph, St. by Billingsgate	278	266	3	55
Bride's, St. Fleet Street / Ditto, Ground in Farringdon Street	6,126	1,472	130	427
*Bridewell Chapel	529	2,400	10	20
Broadway Chapel of Ease to St. Margaret's and St. John	..	7,220	500	335
Catherine, St. Coleman Street	322	388	36	449
Catherine, St. Cree, or Christchurch	1,740	1,100	100	440
*Chapel Royal, Tower	..	525	4	37
Charlton Church	..	2,150	30	68
Chelsea Hospital Burial-ground	Vide St. Luke.	6,696	55	40
Chelsea Old Church		1,210	6	24
Christ Church, Blackfriars Road	..	8,448	520	298
Christ Church, Newgate Street	2,446	1,934	30	75
Christ Church, Spitalfields	20,436	6,413	350	264
Clement, St. Danes	15,459	1,736	100	279
Clement, St. Danes, 2nd Ground, Portugal Street	..	1,422	300	1,021
Cripplegate Poor-ground, Warwick-place, St. Luke's	..	1,400	100	346
Dionis, St. Backchurch	806	132	20	733
Dunstan, St. Fleet Street	3,266	851	208	1,182
Dunstan, St. in the East	1,010	600	150	1,210
Dunstan, St. Stepney	63,723	21,795	200	44
East India Company's Chapel Yard, High Street Poplar	..	6,447	60	45
Edmund, St. the King	391	164	'Seldom used.'	..
Ethelburga, St.	669	240	30	605

* Extra-Parochial.

Parochial

PLACES OF BURIAL.	Population in 1841.	Extent in Square Yards.	Number of Burials.	Burials per Acre.
Fulham Church	9,319	12,000	200	81
George's, St. Bloomsbury	16,981	12,100	300	120
George, St. Botolph Lane	235	76	2	127
George's, St. District Church, Camberwell	39,868	11,640	100	42
George, St. Hanover Square, Burial-ground, Uxbridge Road	66,453	24,200	1,200	240
George, St. in the East	41,350	15,000	500	161
George, St. the Martyr	Vide St. Andrew's.	12,100	200	80
George, St. Burial-ground, Old Kent Road	46,644	1,368	130	460
George, St. the Martyr, Southwark		4,050	470	562
Giles, St. Camberwell	39,868	16,000	500	151
Giles, St. Cripplegate	13,255	4,700	200	206
Giles, St. in the Fields	37,311	4,958	400	390
Ditto, Burial-ground, St. Pancras	..	24,200	1,560	312
Greenwich Church	29,755	2,740	700	1,236
*Greenwich Hospital Burial-ground	..	22,480	300	65
Gregory, St. by St. Paul's	1,444	1,095	100	442
Grosvenor Chapel, South Audley Street	..	6,000	36	29
*Guy's Hospital Ground, Snow's Fields	..	3,120	85	132
Hackney, South	Vide St. John	3,300	100	145
Hackney, West		6,534	200	148
Helen, St. Great	659	779	30	186
Holy Trinity, Brompton	0,515	26,524	100	18
Islington Chapel of Ease	..	17,659	416	114
James, St. Chapel of Ease, Clerkenwell	..	3,500	350	484
James, St. Clerkenwell	56,756	2,000	400	968
James, St. Burial-ground, Ray Street, Clerkenwell	..	800	150	907
James, St. Clerkenwell, 2nd Ground	..	1,000	300	1,452
James, St. Duke's Place	964	338	15	215
James, St. Garlickhithe	520	162	20	598
James, St. New Church	..	8,100	260	155
James, St. Piccadilly	..	4,840	60	60
Ditto, Burial-ground, Hampstead Road	..	26,620	624	113
John, St. Baptist, Savoy	414	600	50	403
John's, St. Chapel of Ease	..	26,000	1,560	290
John's, St. Chapel, Walworth	..	6,400	150	113
John's, St. Church, Waltham Green	..	3,600	15	20
John's, St. Clerkenwell	Vide St. James	315	200	3,073
Ditto, Burial-ground, Benjamin Street	..	1,079	12	54
John, St. the Evangelist	108	7,260	500	333
John, St. the Evangelist, Horslydown	..	9,740	250	124
John, St. the Evangelist, Great Waterloo Street	..	5,924	400	327
John's, St. Hackney	37,771	31,000	700	108
John, St. the Baptist	367	363	12	160
John, St. High Street, Wapping	4,108	6,600	250	183
John's, St. Hoxton	..	6,050	600	480
John, St. Zachary	183	905	6	32

* Private.

Parochial

PLACES OF BURIAL.	Population in 1841.	Estimated Extent in Sq. Yards.	Annual Number of Burials.	No. of Burials per Acre.
King's Road, Chelsea	..	4,840	130	130
Lawrence, St. Jewry	625	200	35	847
Leonard's, St. Ground, Hackney Road	..	2,000	225	544
Leonard's, St. Shoreditch	83,432	8,000	300	181
Luke's, St. Burial-ground, Bath Street	..	1,240	200	781
Luke, St. Chelsea, New Church	40,179	19,360	468	117
Luke's, St. Old Street	49,829	9,287	500	261
Magnus, St.	239	44	6	660
Margaret's. St.	..	5,000	50	48
Margaret, St. Lothbury	189	291	12	300
Margaret, St. Pattens, with	553	81	'Closed'	..
St. Gabriel, Fenchurch Street	..	473	4	41
Mark's, St. Kennington	..	8,960	500	270
Martin, St. in the Fields, Burial-ground, Camden Town	..	19,360	832	208
Ditto, Burial-ground, Drury Lane	..	1,269	40	153
Martin, St. Orgars	353	99	'Seldom used'	..
Martin, St. Outwich	135	123	12	472
Martin, St. Vintry	288	450	3	32
Mary, St. Abbotts, Kensington	26,834	6,620	330	241
Mary, St. Abchurch, with St. Lawrence Pountney	907	566	6	51
Mary, St. Aldermanbury	751	313	30	464
Mary's, St. Burial-ground	..	2,776	200	349
Mary, St. Aldermary	494	173	8	224
Mary, St. at Hill	987	167	40	1,159
Mary, St. at Bow	..	2,716	52	93
Mary, St. Chapel, Hammersmith	..	8,960	20	11
Mary, St. Haggerstone	..	7,260	100	67
Mary, St. Lambeth	115,888	2,400	250	504
Mary, St. Islington	55,690	7,450	750	487
Mary, St. le-Strand, Burial-ground, Russell Court	..	473	90	921
Mary, St. le-Strand	2,520	200	12	290
Mary, St. Love Lane	..	100	'Seldom used'	..
Mary Magdalen, St.	..	288	12	202
Mary Magdalen, St. Bermondsey	34,947	9,184	600	316
Mary's, St. Newington	54,606	8,160	350	208
Mary's, St. Paddington	25,173	20,116	936	222
Mary's, St. Rotherhithe, and	13,917	11,800	345	139
Trinity District Church	..	200		
Mary, St. Somerset	375	389	'Seldom used'	..
Mary, St. Staining	268	423	..	..
Mary's, St. Stoke Newington	..	3,000	50	81
Mary's, St. Whitechapel	34,053	4,219	150	172
Ditto, Workhouse-ground	..	2,776	200	349
Mary, St. Woolnoth	317	33	'Very few'	..
Mary, St. Woolwich	25,785	12,800	600	227
Mary-le-bone, St.	138,164	13,500	520	186
Mary-le-bone, St. Old Church, High Street	138,164	2,000	36	87
Mary-le-Bow, St.	346	250	30	581
Matthew, St. Bethnal Green	74,088	12,100	600	240
Matthew, St. Friday Street	160	208	21	489
Michael, St. Bassishaw	687	222	30	654
Michael, St. Cornhill	454	240	6	121
Michael, St. Queenhithe	647	266	30	342
Ditto, Burial-ground, Trinity Lane	..	158		
Mildred, St. Bread Street	351	242	'Seldom used'	..

Parochial

PLACES OF BURIAL.	Population in 1841.	Estimated Extent in Square Yards.	Annual Number of Burials.	No. of Burials per Acre.
Mildred, St. Poultry	280	84	..	..
Nicholas, St. Acon	194	287	..	..
Nicholas, St. Cole Abbey	254	67	'Never used'	..
Nicholas, St. Olave	431	334	20	290
Pancras, St. Old Church	129,763	24,200	400	80
Paradise Row Burying-ground	..	8,532	1,040	590
Paul's, St. Cathedral	..	3,745	'Seldom used'	..
Paul's, St. Covent Garden	5,718	4,064	200	129
Ditto, Burial-ground contiguous to Workhouse	..	3,455		
Paul's, St. Deptford	..	12,000	360	145
Paul's, St. Hammersmith	9,888	6,888	200	141
Paul's, St. Shadwell	10,060	3,000	250	403
Penitentiary Burial Ground	..	432	10	112
Peter, St. Cheap, corner of Wood St.	227	96	'Never used'	..
Peter, St. Cornhill	656	287	40	674
Peter, St. District Church, Walworth	..	7,800	300	186
Peter-le-Poor, St.	559	48	'Seldom used'	..
Peter's, St. New Church, Hammersmith	3,565	1,210	50	200
Peter, St. Paul's Wharf	341	292	'Seldom used'	..
Poplar New Church	20,342	14,686	300	99
Olave, St. Hart Street	816	462	36	377
Olave, St. Jewry	168	306	'Seldom used'	..
Olave, St. Silver Street	972	335	'Never used'	..
Olave's, St. Tooley Street	6,745	770	200	1,257
Saviour's, St.	18,219	2,700	244	143
Ditto, Cross Bones Ground, Red Cross Street	..	4,500		
Ditto, College Park Street	..	1,040		
Sepulchre, St.	..	1,746	256	293
Ditto, in Church Lane	12,325	1,785		
Ditto, in Durham Yard	..	702		
Stephen, St. Walbrook	322	306	50	791
Swithin's, St. Cannon Street	389	241	20	402
Ditto, 2nd Ground	..	66	24	1,760
Temple Church, St. Mary's	..	400	'Very few'	..
Thomas Apostle, St.	648	340	'Seldom used'	..
Thomas, St. Hospital Ground, Snow's Fields	..	1,449	84	282
Trinity Church, Minories	579	302	7	112
Vedast, St.	427	108		179

Parochial

PLACES OF BURIAL.	Estimated Extent in Sq. Yards.	Annual Number of Burials.	No. of Burials per Acre.
Episcopalians.			
St. Leonard's, Chapel, Bromley	270	52	932
St. George's, Chapel, New Road	3,250	125	186
Presbyterians.			
Gravel Pit Chapel, Hackney	3,300	100	147
St. Andrew's, Scotch Church	900	100	538
Congregationalists or Independents.			
Independent Chapel, Greenwich	1,000	100	484
Pulling's Chapel, Deptford	400	50	605
Wickliffe Chapel, Stepney	600	150	1,210
Ebenezer Chapel, Shadwell	680	120	854
Dr. Burder's, Hackney	3,168	100	153
Meeting House, Old Gravel Lane	60	4	323
Esher Street, Lambeth	1,210	72	288
Brunswick Chapel, Three Colts Street	480	52	524
Collier's Rents, Borough	970	50	249
Abney Chapel, Stoke Newington	780	36	223
Mile End Chapel	2,420	52	104
Trinity Chapel, Poplar	1,200	36	145
Stockwell Green	725	'Very few'	..
Baptists.			
Enon Chapel, Woolwich	112	25	1,080
Worship Street Chapel	720	30	202
Regent Street, Lambeth	320	12	181
Cox's, Dr., Chapel, Hackney	824	26	153
Maze Pond	650	10	74
East Street Chapel	140	2	69
Hammersmith	2,420	30	60
Wesleyan Methodists.			
Methodist Chapel, Woolwich	1,226	100	395
City Road Chapel	2,148	150	338
Stafford Street, Peckham	336	16	230
Wesleyan Chapel, Hammersmith	2,430	18	36
Southwark Chapel, Long Lane, Borough	780	'Very few'	..
Roman Catholics.			
Parker Row, Dockhead	300	100	1,613
Moorfields	120	30	1,210
Poplar	833	140	813
Quakers.			
Long Lane, Bermondsey	2,728	60	106
Coleman Street	4,759	35	35
Hammersmith	1,210	1 or 2	6

Protestant Dissenters' burial grounds and others

PLACES OF BURIAL.	Estimated Extent in Sq. Yards.	Annual Number of Burials.	No of Burials per Acre.
Jews.			
Mile End Road	4,840	52	52
North Street, Mile End Road	24,200	200	40
Chelsea	4,800	22	22
Grove Street	10,890	30	13
Foreign.			
Swedish Chapel	450	10	108
Undescribed.			
Union Chapel, Woolwich	1,500	100	323
Cannon Street Road	2,400	550	1,109
Paradise Row, Lambeth	8,532	1,040	590
New Bunhill Fields, Islington	4,300	520	585
Ebenezer Chapel, Long Lane	265	20	365
Bunhill Fields	18,150	600	160
Zion Chapel, High Street, Borough	210	2	46
Poplar Chapel	8,000	52	31
Maberly Chapel	270	3	54
Brook Street, Ratcliffe Highway	700	2 or 3	21
Millyard Chapel	960	1	5
Whitfield's Chapel, St. Pancras	4,650	300	312
York Street Chapel, Lock's Fields	1,860	'Very few'	..
Denmark Row, Cold Harbour Lane	400	..	..
Salem Chapel, Woolwich	360	'Seldom any'	..
Little Alie Street, Goodman's Fields	'Small'	6	..

GENERAL BURIAL-GROUNDS.

PLACES OF BURIAL.	Estimated Extent in Sq. Yards.	Annual Number of Burials.	No. of Burials per Acre.
*Bunhill Fields, City	8,000	1,000	605
*Bunhill Fields, New	3,250	1,560	2,323
*John's, St. Borough	1,440	142	477
*London, North East	24,200	250	50
*Sheen's New Ground	9,680	600	300
*Spa Fields	14,520	1,560	520

* Private.

CEMETERIES.

PLACES OF BURIAL.	Estimated Extent in Sq. Yards.	Annual Number of Burials.	No. of Burials per Acre.
Highgate Cemetery	101,640	220	10
Nunhead ditto	242,000	208	4
East London ditto, Beaumont Square, Mile End	26,620	850	154
City of London and Tower Hamlets ditto, Mile End	135,520	624	22
West of London and Westminster ditto, Earls Court, Brompton	193,600	254	6
South Metropolitan ditto, Norwood	193,600	180	5
Kensal Green, All Souls' Cemetery	222,640	800	17
Abney Park Cemetery	145,200	200	7

Protestant Dissenters' burial grounds and others

FURTHER READING

Black, Gerry (2003). *Jewish London: an illustrated history* (2003).

Brickley, M., Miles, A., *et al*, 'The Cross Bones burial ground, Redcross Way, Southwark, London: archaeological excavations (1991-1998) for the London Underground Limited Jubilee Line Extension Project'. Museum of London Archaeology Service and Jubilee Line Extension Project.

Chadwick, Edwin, *Report on the practice of Interments in Towns* (1842).

Defoe, Daniel, *A journal of the plague year* (1722, 1990 edition).

Evelyn, John and De Beer, E.S. *et al*, *The diary of John Evelyn* (2006 edn).

Gavin, Hector, *Sanitary Ramblings; being sketches and illustrations of Bethnal Green. A type of the condition of the Metropolis and other large towns* (1848).

Hackman, Harvey, *Wates' book of London churchyards: a guide to the old churchyards and burial-grounds of the City and Central London* (1981).

Harding, Vanessa, 'Burial of the plague dead in early modern London', in *Epidemic Disease in London* (1993), pp 53-64.

Harding, Vanessa, *The dead and the living in Paris and London, 1500-1670* (2002).

Hill and Frere, *Memorials of Stepney Parish* (1890).

Holmes, Isabella (Mrs Basil Holmes), *The London Burial Grounds. Notes on their history from the earliest times to the present day* (1896).

Howarth, G. and Jupp, P., *The changing face of death: historical accounts of death and disposal* (1997).

Kent, William, *The Lost treasures of London* (1947).

Knight, Charles, *London* (1841).

Mackinder, A., 'A Romano-British cemetery on Watling Street: excavations at 165 Great Dover Street, Southwark, London'. Museum of London Archaeology Service (2000).

Maitland, William *The History of London from its foundation by the Romans to the present time...* (1739).

Meteyard, E. *The Hallowed Spots of Ancient London ....* (1861).

Pennant, Thomas, *Some account of London, Westminster and Southwark* (1813).

Pepys, Samuel, ed J. Smith *et al*, *The Diary of Samuel Pepys* (1943 edn).

Richardson, Ruth, *Death, dissection and the destitute* (1987).

Stow, John and Morley, H., *A survey of London: written in the year* 1598 (1994 edn).

Timbs, John, *Curiosities of London: exhibiting the most rare and remarkable objects of interest in the Metropolis, London* (1855).

The Victoria County History of London.

Walker, George A., *Gatherings from Grave Yards* (1839).

Walker, George A., *Burial-ground Incendiarism. The last fire at the Bone-House in the Spa Fields Golgotha ...* (1846).

Woollacott, Ron, *Southwark's Burying Places.*

Ziegler, Philip, *The Black Death* (1970).

Probably the definitive website on the subject see http://www.doubleo.fsnet.co.uk.

WALK ONE
The East End of London

Vallance Gardens, St Mary's Additional Ground, St Mary Matfelon's church. *Allow 90 minutes.*

Start at Vallance Gardens, a large open space in Vallance Road E1. This ground was described by Holmes as being about an acre, which was acquired by Quakers in 1687. The ground was formerly known as Baker's Row, and as can be seen from Illustration 136, taken in 1896, it still retains much of its original layout. The ground was closed for burials in 1857.

From Vallance Gardens cross the road heading west into Old Montague Street, for St Mary's Additional Ground. Estate Road is on the left. Walk in, and the burial ground is the large green area on your left. Note the height of the ground above pavement level, and the ominous looking mounds and contours. A workhouse was built here in 1768 on the site of a former graveyard, and the open area was consecrated in 1796 for burials. The ground was closed in 1853 and it is likely that burials extend under many of the surrounding buildings. Holmes tells us that 'in 1832 196 cholera cases were interred in the joining piece of ground ...' This ground was stated by Walker in 1839 to be 'as thickly crowded with the remains of the dead as the burying ground adjoining to the church'. In 2005 human remains were found at the nearby Davenant Centre, at 179-181 Whitechapel Road.

On leaving Estate Road, turn left into Old Montague Street, and then left into Davenant Street. On reaching Whitechapel Road, turn right. Approximately 200 metres on the left, on the other side of the road, is a large walled area, which used to contain the 14th-century church of St Mary Matfelon. It is now called Altab Ali Park. Enter the ground and you will see some tombstones to your right, and ahead. Walk straight ahead and you will see the chalked outline of the last church. This ground was the last resting place of Richard Brandon, who it is believed executed Charles I in 1649. Walker in 1839 said of this ground, which fronted 'one of the greatest thoroughfares in London' that it was 'so densely crowded as to present one entire mass of human bones and putrefaction ... coffin wood is plentifully strewed over the ground in a rotten and decomposed state ...' The church was destroyed by bombing in 1940 and was demolished entirely in 1952.

On leaving the ground walk east along Whitechapel Road heading towards the London Hospital - distinctive from the heli-pad and helicopter usually parked on its roof. After 500 metres, on reaching New Road turn right. Approximately 200 metres on the left is Newark Street. On the corner of Newark and Turner Streets is St Philip's church, on the site of a 1665 plague burial ground. Holmes says that a large area to the south of the hospital was a burial ground, and that 'quite an acre and a half was the burial ground' where unclaimed corpses from the London Hospital found their last resting place. The parallel street to Newark Street, a few metres to the north, is Stepney Way which used to be called Oxford Street. It was along here, on the right, that the former nurses' tennis court lay (*see illustration 29*) where coffined burials often led to the ground giving way under the nurses' feet.

WALK TWO
The East End of London

Jewish cemeteries, Globe Road, Bancroft Almshouses. *Allow 2 hours*

This walk starts at Bancroft Road E1, on the corner which is part of the Queen Mary campus of the University of London. Walk up Bancroft Road and turn left into Alderney Road. A couple of hundred metres along, straight ahead, you will see tall, dark walls protected by glass shards on the top. To the right is a small entrance door. This Jewish cemetery dates from 1697, and prior to that was a plot of garden land belonging to a Captain Nathaniel Owen. It was this cemetery which once featured a moveable wheeled sentry box from which congregation members armed with blunderbusses guarded new burials against the 'Resurrection men'. The cemetery closed in 1852. The ground can be peeked at through a letterbox in the door, but normally one needs to phone the United Synagogue to make an appointment to enter this quite extensive and very interesting ground, which is looked after by an on-site resident caretaker.

On leaving the cemetery continue to the end of Alderney Road and then turn right into Globe Road. After approximately 350 metres you will reach a railway bridge. We here are at the former Globe Road burial ground and it was from this spot that in 1839 a Mr Poole, an employee of the Eastern Counties Railway Company stood on the bridge and observed 'two men and a boy exhuming the bodies buried in one part of the ground, and hurling them, in the most indecent manner ...' and called the police who 'met a lad with a bag of bones ...' and in a corner of the the ground 'found there a great number of bodies, packed one upon another, in a very deep grave which had been dug to receive them, and the uppermost coffin was not more than seven or eight inches, at the utmost from the surface. The remaining part of this once appalling private venture burial ground stands on the right, on the corner of Globe Road and Portman Place. There is a sign calling the ground 'Globe Road Memorial Gardens.' The ground opened in 1820, and possibly contains 14,000 burials, though some have been lost under the buildings between what survives and the railway bridge. The ground is usually locked but this is no hindrance as the full extent of this dilapidated cemetery can be seen from the pavement. The ground during the 1830s emitted a dreadful stench.

Walk back along Globe Road and turn left into Bancroft Road, and after about 500 metres on the left is the Bancroft Road Jewish cemetery, visible from the pavement, and still showing signs of being struck by a bomb during World War II. The ground was first used in 1811, but by 1884 showed signs of neglect. In 2008 it is run down and derelict.

Continue along Bancroft Road until you reach Whitechapel Road and turn left towards the former site of the People's Palace, which is now the main entrance area of the Queen Mary campus. To the western side of the campus, nearest to Bancroft Road, lie some neglected tombstones in the bushes next to the pavement fronting Whitechapel Road. These are from the former burial ground of the Bancroft Almshouses, founded in 1727 and demolished *c*. 1884. Holmes describes in 1896 much that remains in 2008: '... there is a piece open to the road ... there are, at any rate, four gravestones left, against the wall ... I daresay it is only a very small proportion of those who pass in and out of the Palace who have ever noticed this relic of the Bancroft Almshouses.' Also, to the western side of the campus behind a large wall, and best observed by making an appointment first, is the Old Velho Sephardi Jewish cemetery. It is located directly behind Albert Stern House, at 253 Mile End Road. Enter the campus area. On the eastern side, is a large cemetery, the Novo Beth Chaim Jewish cemetery, which was opened in 1724. This is next to the Faculty of Arts building.

WALK THREE
Around Finsbury

Bunhill Fields, Wesley Chapel, Golden Lane. *Allow two hours.*

This walk commences in City Road at Bunhill Fields. The burial ground was consecrated in 1665 and almost certainly used for plague burials. There are a number of famous persons buried amongst the estimated 120,000 bodies, including William Blake, John Bunyan and Daniel Defoe. On leaving the ground again at the City Road entrance, directly opposite is Wesley's Chapel, which plays host to a free museum. Directly behind the Chapel is a burial ground over which an office block has been built, leading to tombstones emerging from the concrete. This ground is unusual and worth visiting (*see ills. 116 and 117*).

On leaving the WesleyChapel, walk north to the nearby Old Street roundabout and go left into Old Street. After 200 metres you will reach Bath Street on the north side of the road. This road was the site of a pesthouse which is commemorated by a plaque, easily visible on a red brick building to your left. On the right, almost opposite is the St Luke's Estate. Fronting the road is a large modernistic style playground and cut-through. This was the burial ground for the pesthouse which was consecrated in1662. (*See ills. 109 and 110*).

Go back down Bath Street into Old Street, turn right and walk west for 200 metres until you reach St Luke's church. The crypt is now used by the London Symphony Orchestra. Walker in 1839 said of this churchyard that it emitted 'effluvia' to an 'alarming extent', and that the vaults beneath the church were 'particularly offensive'. The vaults were cleared in the 1990s.

Continue along Old Street for around 200 metres and turn left into Golden Lane. On the left you will come to a Peabody Estate. The central area of the estate is where the Cripplegate Poor Ground lies. It was first used in 1636 and was very overcrowded. A short walk further down Golden Lane will bring you to Fortune Street Park. Just beyond the park is Prior Weston school where the Golden Lane burial ground was sited. Nearly 10,000 bodies were recently exhumed from this site. Almost opposite the school, walk into Fann Street, and past the traffic barrier. At the end of the road you will see a compact, open space with a sign which reads 'Fann Street Wildlife Garden'. This is part of the former Cupid Court burial ground which was shown on the 1871 Ordnance Survey. Then proceed back to Golden Lane and turn north again in the direction of Old Street.

About 200 metres on the right is Banner Street. Walk into this and on the right you will see a street sign pointing to the Friends' burial ground which is still very much as described by Holmes in 1896. There is a memorial building, a small park, and a playground with a number of memorials. This well-hidden and atmospheric ground dates from 1661.

WALK FOUR

Theatre-land and Aldwych area.

Drury Lane, Clare Market, Enon Chapel. *Allow 2 hours.*

Begin at Inigo Jones' St Paul's church in the middle of Covent Garden, part of whose burial area has been paved over. In 1839 Walker said of this ground that a gravedigger had told him that 'on several occasions, he had been driven from the attempt of digging a grave, and compelled to throw back the earth, owing to the dangerous effluvia he experienced from the soil'. And that the vault underneath the church was also crowded.

Walk east through the old market into Russell Street, keep the Theatre Royal to the right and turn left into Drury Lane. Around 100 metres on your left you will come to the Drury Lane Gardens, a former additional burial ground for St Martin-in-the-Fields. This seemingly innocuous ground was one of London's worst. In 1839 Walker said that it was saturated with dead and that the number of burials meant the height of the ground was level with the first floor windows of surrounding houses. Pits were dug for bodies, and covered by boards until full. It is likely that this is the churchyard described by Dickens in *Bleak House*. As you enter the ground you will see the old watch house on the right, and mortuary building. Much of the ground is now a play area but some worn down tombstones remain. For a true idea of the level of burials in this ground, walk down Crown Court and see the height of the entrance to the ground on the right.

Approximately 200 metres on the right is the site of the former Russell Court burial ground which was described by Holmes as comprising 430 square yards ... 'It is probable that few grounds in London were more overcrowded with bodies than this one.' Closed in 1853, its location is pinpointed by a double gate next door to a seafood bar. Walk back down Drury Lane and left into Aldwych, continuing into Kingsway. Turn right into Portugal Street and walk east.Where the road meets Carey Street, on the site of the LSE library building was the notorious 'Green Ground'. Walker in 1839 visited this and wrote '... several bones were lying on the surface of the grave nearest to us ...' The overall state of this ground was appallingly gruesome, and unhygienic.'

Walk down along the Clare Market section of the LSE campus passing Waterstone's on your left, and walk for approximately 200 metres until you reach a set of concrete stairs leading down towards the Law Courts. At the top of the steps on your left is Grange Court which is dominated by a round building, the St Clement's Building. On this site once stood the notorious Enon Chapel, a private burial vault with a place of worship above, which opened in 1822 and caused a scandal. It was on this spot that in a space of 60 feet by 29 and 6 feet deep some 12,000 bodies were interred. When the St Clement's Building was erected in 1967, a large quantity of human bones was uncovered. With the St Clement's Building behind you, walk down the steps. Approximately 100 metres ahead of you are the Royal Courts of Justice. Facing the entrance to the courts, the area next to the car park on your left, with a couple of benches, is a former almshouse burial ground, which came into use in 1802. Walker said of this that it was 'filled with the dead; many of the coffins being near the surface. Behind you in the centre of the Strand is the church of St Clement Danes, well worth a visit for the crypt (*ill. 67*) which at the end of the 18th century was overcrowded with the dead, and reeked of decomposition. Walking back along the Strand towards Drury Lane is St Mary-le-Strand in the middle of the road. At one time its burial ground, now mostly under the road, was so overcrowded that the local well was polluted. Walking down the north side of the church on the pavement you will see the various burial vaults listed on the wall of the church.

INDEX

INDEX